The Magical
Math
Book

BOB LONGE

Sterling Publishing Co., Inc.
New York

Sterling Books by Bob Longe

Easy Card Tricks
Easy Magic Tricks
Great Card Tricks
The Magical Math Book
Mind Reading Magic Tricks
Mystifying Card Tricks
Nutty Challenges & Zany Dares
101 Amazing Card Tricks
World's Best Card Tricks
World's Best Coin Tricks
World's Greatest Card Tricks

Library of Congress Cataloging -in-Publication Data

Longe, Bob, 1928-
    Magical math book / Bob Longe.
        p.   cm.
    Includes index.
    Summary: Explains how to use well-concealed mathematical prin-
ciples to perform all kinds of magic tricks.
        ISBN 0-8069-9989-6
        1. Tricks--Juvenile literature. 2. Conjuring--Juvenile literature.
3. Mathematical recreations-- Juvenile literature. [1. Magic tricks.
2. Mathematical recreations.] I. Title
GV1548.L59 1997
793.8'01'51—dc21   97–33100
                                                          CIP
                                                          AC

10 9 8 7 6 5 4 3 2 1

First paperback edition published in 1998 by
Sterling Publishing Company, Inc.
387 Park Avenue South, New York, N.Y. 10016
© 1997 by Bob Longe
Distributed in Canada by Sterling Publishing
% Canadian Manda Group, One Atlantic Avenue, Suite 105
Toronto, Ontario, Canada M6K 3E7
Distributed in Great Britain and Europe by Cassell PLC
Wellington House, 125 Strand, London WC2R 0BB, England
Distributed in Australia by Capricorn Link (Australia) Pty Ltd.
P.O. Box 6651, Baulkham Hills, Business Centre, NSW 2153, Australia
Manufactured in the United States of America
All rights reserved

Sterling ISBN 0-8069-9989-6 Trade
              0-8069-9990-X Paper

CONTENTS

INTRODUCTION 5

FOR THE AGES 7

Of an Age 7

Phone It In 9

Birthday Change 10

More Info 12

Age and Address, Please 14

Old Enough 15

BAFFLING TRICKS 17

A Sly Inference 17

The Easy Way 19

Hummer by Phone 21

Getting Along 23

Children and Other Pets 24

CARDS 26

Five Chosen Cards 26

Invisible Deck—Again 28

Unlucky Seven 30

Two Are Better Than One 32

Double-Surprise 34

Simple Miraskill 38

DICE 42

The Dice Are Cast 42

Have a Roll 43

Take Two 44

Talk 'n' Roll 45

MIND READING 46

Working Together 46

And the Number Is... 48

A Good Call 51

A Little Help 52

Play the Odds 53

PREDICTION **55**

Magician's Choice 55

Tallying the Future 56

BOOK TESTS **58**

Completely by Chance 58

Odds or Evens 60

FUN STUFF **63**

It All Adds Down 63

Please State Your City 64

Still Hungry? 64

All Together Now 65

A Nickel for Your Thoughts 65

The Sneaky Serpent 66

LIGHTNING CALCULATION **69**

The Speedy Adder 69

An Additional Trick 73

MEMORY TRICKS **79**

Serial Number Scam 79

Ah, Yes, I Remember It Well 80

As I Recall 82

MAGIC SQUARES **84**

An Easy Square 84

On the Square 87

So Where's the Money? **91**

MASTERY LEVELS CHART & INDEX **94**

ABOUT THE AUTHOR **96**

INTRODUCTION

One purpose of this book is to use a wide variety of mathematical principles in presenting demonstrations that appear to be magic. In all of these tricks, the mathematical principle is well-concealed. In fact, in many of them the use of numbers is not even suspected.

Too often, I think, performers treat tricks involving numbers as puzzles rather than magic. It's easy enough, then, for a spectator to say to himself, "I don't know exactly how it's done, but I know that it's just mathematics." Your job is to keep this from happening. Thoughtful patter can turn nearly any trick into magic. For instance:

1) "As you know, through the years many people have felt that certain numbers have magical qualities. Seven is supposed to be lucky; and thirteen is supposed to be unlucky. Also, the number three is said to be quite mystical. If there is something magical about numbers, I'd like to take advantage of it. So let's use numbers in this experiment."

2) "Numbers surround us. What page? How old? What date? How tall? When? And so on. Since numbers are so common, it seems appropriate that we try to work some magic with them."

3) "For this experiment, we could use words or symbols or pictures. I prefer to use numbers."

4) "Everyone seems to have a favorite number, even several favorite numbers. Perhaps we can use one of these numbers to accomplish something magical."

5) "Since we're all familiar with numbers, it seems appropriate to try a magical experiment with them."

For most of the tricks, I've provided additional patter ideas. Undoubtedly, other ideas will occur to you, depending on the nature of the trick.

Many of the mathematical principles used in this book are explained early on in various simple tricks. As you proceed, you can see how these principles are applied in different ways to other tricks. Thus, you are provided something of a sequential approach to these principles while learning entertaining tricks.

Because I thought it was important to introduce certain principles early, you'll find that, by and large, later tricks are more "magical" than earlier tricks.

The vast majority of these tricks are followed by an explanation called *Why It Works*. This is designed not only to help you better understand the principle behind the trick, but also to enable you to consider alterations to the trick or to develop other tricks of your own.

For many of these tricks, I assume that you have provided the volunteer with a writing implement and paper, or a calculator. I prefer that the spectator do math with pencil (or pen) and paper. This helps build suspense. And if you're unsure of a spectator's math ability, you can have another volunteer help. In other words, they perform the math together. (It's insulting to have someone else actually check the work.)

As for the individual tricks, you'll perform extraordinary effects with cards, dice, and pencil and paper. You'll read minds, make accurate predictions, discover a person's age. Also, you'll show the power of your brain by performing lightning-quick calculations, constructing apparently complex "magic squares," and demonstrating your remarkable memory in a variety of ways.

No sleight of hand is used, but misdirection, clever presentation, and other subtleties ensure that the spectators are completely flummoxed.

Enjoy!

FOR THE AGES

Over the years, magicians and mathematicians have developed many sneaky ways to determine a person's age. Here we have six methods for accomplishing this, plus ways to elicit all sorts of other information.

In each instance, a spectator performs a number of mathematical procedures, finally announcing to you the total. A spectator might wonder, "If you're really performing magic, why don't you simply tell the spectator's age without all this foolishness?"

One way to stifle this speculation is to present these tricks as mind reading. "It's impossible for me to read someone's mind without some sort of aid. Often, various procedures with numbers will enable me to discover certain facts." Then proceed. Obviously, anyone with sense will know that it's all baloney. Still, there might be a small doubt. Regardless, the mind-reading approach adds to the fun.

If you use this approach, be sure to concentrate as you slowly deliver the proper information.

Of an Age

Ask Myrna, your unwitting dupe, to write down any number. (For convenience, you may want to restrict it to no more than three digits.) She may, of course, use a calculator.

"Multiply this number by 9," you say, "for 9 is a mystic number."

Let's assume she writes down 532. She multiplies this by 9, giving her 4788.

"Add your age to that number, please."

She adds 26, giving her 4814.

"I can't possibly know the original number you chose, nor your age. But to get our minds in tune, I must know the final number you wrote down."

Myrna tells you 4814. You must mentally add the digits, and keep adding the resulting digits, until you end up with a single digit. You have 4814, so you add these digits together: 4+8+1+4=17.

You still have two digits, so you add these together: 1+7=8.

So you have reduced the number to 8. Myrna's age will be a multiple of 9 plus the digit you have come up with—in this case, 8. So you must guess a bit. Does she look 17 (1×9+8)? No. How about 26 (2×9+8)? That's a possibility. How about 35 (3×9+8)? No, she seems younger than that. So 26 it is. You tell Myrna her age.

Other evidence can make your guess easier. What is the general age category of the group, for example? Or what is the age category of the other ladies she has been chatting with? Did she go to school with someone whose age you know?

Let's try another example. This time, you'll work with Myrna's mother, Agatha. "Think of a number, Agatha, and jot it down." She writes down 683.

"Multiply that by 9." 683×9=6147

"Add your age, please." She adds 55: 6147+55=6202.

You ask her to tell you the final number. When you hear that it's 6202, you add the digits: 6+2+0+2=10.

You add the 1 and 0: 1+0=1.

Agatha's age will be a multiple of 9 plus the digit you end up with—in this instance, 1.

Does Agatha look 37 (4×9+1)? No, she doesn't. Besides, she has a 26-year-old daughter. How about 46 (5×9+1)? No, she looks somewhat older than that. How about 55 (6×9+1)? That seems to be just about right. So 55 it is.

If you are not sure about the person's age, you will never go wrong guessing the lower age. When told you are mistaken, you can always cover by saying, "I'm sorry. I was going by looks, instead of the mental message you were sending me. Your actual age is 64 (or whatever)."

Why It Works: Since our number system is based on 10, the number 9 is the highest digit in the system. This gives 9 all sorts of unique qualities. For instance, any number multiplied by 9 will have a product whose digits can be reduced to 9.

An example: Let's multiply 3786 by 9. We get a product of 34,074. Add the digits together: 3+4+0+7+4=18.

Again, add the digits together: 1+8=9.

Once more: Any number multiplied by 9 will break down to 9. Nine times 842, for instance, will equal 7578. Add the digits and you get 27. Add the 2 and 7 and you get 9.

Multiply by 9, and you always get 9.

In the above trick, Myrna thinks of a number and multiplies it by 9. For example, she thinks of the number 7 and multiplies this by 9, getting 63. You reduce this to a single digit and get 9. If you subtract 9 from this, you get zero. This will always be true. When Myrna multiplies her original number by 9, she actually eliminates the number, leaving a multiple of 9.

So when she adds in her age and you reduce the result to a single digit, the digit stands for her age, plus a multiple of 9. So you add 9 to the digit. If this doesn't produce a reasonable result, you must keep adding 9 until you get to an age that makes sense.

Notes:

1) If you take any number and multiply it by a number whose digits will reduce to 9, the answer can also be reduced to 9.

2) You may be able to do all the required computing in your head. If not, you may find it convenient to use a pencil and a small pad or a sheet of paper. And I don't think there's a law against your using a calculator.

Phone It In

In this excellent and easy trick, you can determine how long ago an event occurred, or in what year it occurred. The most obvious choice, of course, is age, but it could be the year of a marriage, a prom, discharge from service, whatever.

Perhaps Casper will help out. Tell him, "You'll have to use your imagination here, Casper. I want you to pretend that you're by your telephone, and that you're calling me up to give me a hint as to your age. Please look down at your invisible phone and take special note of your phone number. Pick out any four of the digits in your number and jot them down as a four-digit number." Wait till he finishes. "Mix up those four digits any way you want and jot down a completely different four-digit number which includes those same digits." Pause. "Now, subtract the smaller number from the larger number."

When he has his result, continue: "Now, add up the digits in your answer."

For example, if your answer were 567, you'd add 5 and 6 and 7, getting 18. Make sure Casper understands. "If you still have more than one digit, add the remaining digits together. Keep doing this until you end up with one digit."

Wait. "Add 7 to this."

Wait. "Finally, add to this the last two digits of the year you were born."

Wait. "Tell me the total."

Casper tells you the total. "You know something? That really isn't much of a hint," you say. Still, you promptly tell him his year of birth. Or you might say, "At the end of this year, you'll be (so many) years old." All you do is subtract 16 from Casper's answer, and you have the key year.

How can this be? Easy. When Casper finishes his subtraction, he has the number 9. You tell him to add 7. This gives him 16. He then adds the last two digits of the significant year. To find the year, you just subtract 16.

Let's try a concrete example. Suppose Casper chooses these four digits: 4978. He mixes them up and comes up with this four-digit number: 7489. He subtracts the smaller number from the larger:

$$
\begin{array}{r}
7489 \\
-4978 \\
\hline
2511
\end{array}
$$

He reduces 2511 to a single digit: 2+5+1+1=9.

He adds 7: 9+7=16.

Suppose Casper was born in 1972. He adds in the last two digits: 16+72=88.

He tells you the result. You subtract 16: 88-16=72. So 1972 was his year of birth. If you want his age (or to announce how many years ago the special event took place), subtract the year the event took place from the current year. Say, "At the end of this year, you'll be (so many) years old." Or, "At the end of this year, it will be (so many) years since the event took place."

Why It Works: This is another example of the power of 9. Take any number—61, for instance— shift the digits around, and subtract the smaller digit from the larger one. Then add the resulting digits. The result? A number that will reduce to 9.

$$61-16=45. \quad 4+5=9.$$

Let's try a 3-digit number, 941. Let's move the digits around and subtract from it 419: 941-419=522. 5+2+2=9.

But suppose we subtract from 941 a different combination, 194:

$$941-194=747. \quad 7+4+7=18. \quad 1+8=9.$$

Yes, it works no matter what. The same is true of four-digit numbers, five-digit numbers, and so on. That is why Casper will always get the number 9 when he subtracts. He could, in fact, use his entire phone number instead of just four numbers, but that could get tedious.

This principle makes many number tricks possible. Perhaps you can invent one of your own.

Birthday Change

Let's work with Alfred. Here is a way not only to discover his age, but also to reveal the amount of change he has in his pocket.

First, you need to qualify Alfred. "Do you have more than a dollar's worth of change in your pocket?" you ask him. If he does, this won't work. Either have him reduce the amount of change to less than a dollar, or work with someone else.

. Turn away and provide these directions. "Write down your age, please. Double it. Add 5. Multiply by 50. Count the change in your pocket and add that amount. Add 115."

At this point you can say, "Subtract the number of days in a regular year." With Alfred, you might have to say, "Subtract 365."

The result will be a four-digit number. The first two digits are Alfred's age; the last two are the amount of change he has in his pocket (03 would be three cents).

You can point out this result to the group. I prefer to subtract 365 myself, letting no one see my result, and then announce the age and the amount of change.

Let's review. You turn away and provide these instructions:

1) Write down your age. (Alfred is 23.)

2) Double it: 46.

3) Add 5: 51.

4) Multiply by 50: 2550.

5) Add the amount of change in your pocket: (Alfred has 85 cents. He adds this to 2550, getting 2635.)

6) Add 115: 2750.

7) Subtract the number of days in a regular year — 365: 2385.

The first two digits in this trick give you Alfred's age; the last two digits give you the amount of change he has in his pocket. As I mentioned earlier, I prefer to perform Step 7 myself. This enables me to announce his age and the amount of change he has in his pocket, thus providing more mystery.

Why It Works: This is what I like to refer to as a "give-and-take" trick. You keep adding and subtracting until you end up with a number which you can use to reveal some numerical facts.

To create a similar trick, you start by choosing a birth date and an amount of change. You then throw in several items to raise the total and to create confusion. Included among these items will be the birth date and the amount of change. Finally, you subtract an amount which will bring about the result you're looking for.

Let's try to develop a simplified version of this trick. We'll start with Rita, who is 32 years old and has 63 cents in her purse. So we know exactly what number we want to end up with: 3263.

We can get the number easily. All we have to do is have Rita write-down her age, multiply it by 100, and add in the change she has in her purse.

$$100 \times 32 = 3200. \quad 3200 + 63 = 3263.$$

The trick certainly was easy, but it didn't fool anybody. To be more deceptive, early on we must add in something which we can take out later. In the trick that was described above, the inventor has his assistant double her age and then add 5. Then this total is multiplied by 50. Now, let's try that with Rita.

$$32 \times 2 = 64. \quad 64 + 5 = 69. \quad 69 \times 50 = 3450.$$

Actually, the inventor has, in effect, multiplied the age by 100 and added in 250. The age is multiplied by 2 and then 50, which is the same as multiplying by 100. The 5 that was added to the age is, of course, also multiplied by 50; this gives you the additional 250.

At this point, if you choose, you could have Rita add in the amount of change in her purse. Then to get the desired number, you would subtract 250. This shortened trick would go like this:

1) Write down your age. (Rita is 32.)

2) Double it: 64.

3) Add 5: 69.

4) Multiply by 50: 3450.

5) Add the amount of change in your purse. (Rita adds 63 to 3450, getting 3513.)

At this point, you could ask for the total and mentally subtract 250. (3513−250=3263.) Or you could have Rita do the subtraction. The first two digits are her age, and the last two indicate the amount of change she has.

I hope you've noticed that this version is only one step shorter than the original. The inventor apparently yearned to use the number of days in a year. So he threw in an extra step. We subtracted 250 to get the proper number. But the inventor wanted to subtract 365. Obviously, in a new step, we must throw in an additional amount. If we add 115 to 250, we'll get 365. (365−250=115.) Thus, you get Step 6 in the original trick.

More Info

With this clever trick, you're able to tell a person his age, along with the month and day of the month on which he was born. For this one, you should probably jot down the various steps; they might be a bit hard to remember.

Phyllis would be happy to help you by performing the following steps:

1) Jot down the number of the month you were born. (January is 1, February is 2, March is 3, and so on.)

2) Multiply by 100.

3) Add the day of month of your birth.

4) Multiply by 2.

5) Add 9.

6) Multiply by 5.

7) Add 8.

8) Multiply by 10.

9) Subtract 419.

10) Add your age.

Phyllis tells you the result. You subtract 111. The two digits on the right give Phyllis's age. The two digits to the left of this give the day of the month of her birth. The remaining digits on the left give the month.

Phyllis, for instance, was born on November 4. She follows these steps:

1) She jots down 11 for November.

2) She multiplies by 100: 1100.

3) She adds the day of the month, 4: 1104.

4) She multiplies by 2: 2208.

5) She adds 9: 2217.

6) She multiplies by 5: 11085.

7) She adds 8: 11093.

8) She multiplies by 10: 110930.

9) She subtracts 419: 110511.

10) She adds her age, 16: 110527.

She tells you the result; you subtract 111, getting 110416. The two digits on the right tell you Phyllis is 16. The 04 to the left of these tells you the day of the month on which she was born. The first two digits tell you that she was born in the 11th month, November.

Why It Works: This is another example of a "give-and-take" trick. Phyllis provides the vital information. You have her add and multiply various numbers.

Let's simplify the basic trick. We'll start with Tim, who is 25 and was born on May 13. We need to end with this number: 51325.

Just as in the original, we'll get some of the basic information down in a hurry. Tim writes down the number for the month of his birth (5) and multiplies it by 100, giving him 500. He adds the day of the month, 13, giving him 513. He multiplies this by 2, getting 1026.

To confuse things a bit, you have him add 9 to 1026, to come up with 1035.

This takes us through Step 5 in the original trick. Let's eliminate some steps. For Step 6, Tim now multiplies his total by 50, getting 51750. To this he adds his age, giving him 51775.

In effect, you have again multiplied the month and day by 100. (You first doubled the data, and then multiplied it by 50.) You added 9, which was also multiplied by 50; this added 450 to the total. Finally, Tim added in his age. Tim tells you his total. Clearly, to get the desired result, you need only subtract 450.

$$\begin{array}{r} 51775 \\ -450 \\ \hline 51325 \end{array}$$

If you had wanted to, you could have had Tim subtract a portion of the 450 as a final step, and then you subtract the rest mentally after you get the total.

So here is the shorter trick that we just developed. Tim, who is 25, was born on May 13. He performs the following steps:

1) He jots down 5 for May.
2) He multiplies by 100: 500.
3) He adds the day of the month, 13: 513.
4) He multiplies by 2: 1026.
5) He adds 9: 1035.
6) He multiplies by 50: 51750.
7) He adds his age, 25: 51775.

You are told the total and you subtract 450, getting 51325. The first number tells you Tim was born in May, the next two tell you it was the 13th, and the last two tell you he's 25 years old.

Note: Even if you have the steps jotted down on a slip of paper and are reading them to your helper, it enhances the trick if you pretend to arbitrarily select the numbers you choose. For instance, in the original Step (9), you might say, "All right, now we should have you subtract something. Let's see. How about subtracting...oh...419."

Age and Address, Please

This is one I worked on for quite a while. I'm not sure whether I invented it. Regardless, it provides an easy method for determining a person's age and address.

Ask Charlene to help out. Let's suppose that she's 31 years old and lives at 2979 Brunswick. Provide her with these instructions:

1) Put down your street number: 2979.

2) Double it: 5958.

3) Add 5: 5963.

4) Multiply by 50: 298150.

5) Add your age (31): 298181.

6) Add the number of days in a regular year (365): 298546.

Charlene tells you her result. You subtract 15 from the last two numbers to get her age: 46-15=31.

You subtract 6 from the remaining numbers to get her address: 2985-6=2979.

Suppose Charlene lives at 583 Brunswick Street. Her total would be 58946. You subtract 15 from the last two numbers, again getting 31. The remaining digits are 589. You subtract 6 from 589, coming up with her address, 583.

Why It Works: Like the previous two tricks, this is an example of "give- and-take." As with the previous two tricks, the numbers you subtract are chosen because they bring about the desired results.

Old Enough

The above title refers to the age of the trick itself. Although it's been around a long time, it still works well. Further, its method is quite different from the others we've looked at.

Give Alice these instructions:

1) Jot down your age. (Actually, she can jot down any number.)

2) Multiply it by 3.

3) Add 1 to the total.

4) Multiply by 3.

5) Add the original number.

Then you ask for the total. Suppose that she jots down 23. She multiplies by 3, getting 69. She adds 1, getting 70. She multiplies by 3, getting 210. She adds her original number, getting 233.

When you're told this number, you eliminate the last digit. This gives you 23, which is her original number.

Clearly, you'd have a better trick if you threw in another number. After she multiplies by 3 the second time, you might have her add 20. Her final total now will be 253. Again, you eliminate the last digit, giving you 25. Subtract 2 from that, and you get her original number.

Why It Works: Let's eliminate one of the steps, and I think you'll see exactly how the trick works. We'll eliminate Step 3, where you add 1 to the total. Let's use the number 45.

1) Jot down a number (45).

2) Multiply it by 3. (3×45=135.)

3) Multiply it by 3 again. (3×135=405.)

4) Add the original number. (405+45=450.)

When you drop the last digit, which is zero in this instance, you get 45. So what actually happened? You multiplied by 3 twice, which is the equivalent of multiplying by 9. You add in the original number. So you have now, in effect, multiplied by 10.

In the simplified example above, then, you've done nothing more than multiply the original number by 10. To make it somewhat more mysterious, the inventor of the trick had the spectator add 1 after she first multiplied by 3. Then, when she finished figuring, the first digits would match the original number, but the last digit would be 3.

BAFFLING TRICKS

A Sly Inference

Bob Hummer invented this excellent trick, which, basically, is an exercise in simple logic. Required are three different small objects. In our example, we will assume the objects are a key, a pencil, and a ring.

Lorna is eager to assist, so tell her, "Let's try a test to see if I can discover the one object of three that you are thinking of. We'll use these three objects." Place the three objects in a row on the table. The order doesn't matter. "Lorna, here we have a key, a pencil, and a ring." Let us assume that you have set them on the table so that the key is on your right, the pencil is in the middle, and the ring is on your left. Point to the ring, saying, "Right now the ring is in Position 1." Point to the pencil. "The pencil is in Position 2." Point to the key. "And the key is in Position 3." As you can see, you number the positions so that, from her view, they are in ascending order from left to right; from your view, therefore, they are in descending order from left to right (Illus. 1).

"Lorna, I'll turn my back and then ask you to exchange two of the objects. Now, don't tell me which objects you exchange, just tell me the positions. You might, for instance, change the positions of the ring and the pencil. The ring is in Position 1 and the pencil is in Position 2. Just tell me, 'One and two.'"

Make sure that she understands. Turn your back and tell her to begin. After she exchanges two objects, giving you their original positions, tell

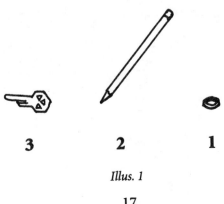

3   2   1

Illus. 1

her, "Now, again exchange any two of the objects, once more telling me which positions you're switching." She continues doing this for as long as she wishes.

When she is done, tell her, "Lorna, simply think of one of the objects. Are you thinking of one? Good. Please remember that object. Now, without telling me anything, switch the positions of the other two objects. In other words, exchange the other two objects."

After she does so, say, "Let's go back to the original procedure. Exchange two objects and tell me which positions you switched." She continues doing this any number of times. When she says she is done, turn and face the group. "Lorna, please concentrate on the object you thought of." You carefully study all three objects. Finally, your hand falls on one of them. "This one," you declare. And, of course, you're right.

You repeat the stunt any number of times to prove that this is not mere coincidence, that you have some sort of extraordinary power. There is no point in telling the group that this extraordinary power is the ability to count on your fingers.

The secret: At the beginning, note the middle object on the table, the one at Position 2. In our example, this is the pencil. Turn your back and hold up the first three fingers of either hand. Mentally, number the fingers 1, 2, and 3. Place your thumb on the middle one of the three fingers, thus marking the pencil as being in Position 2 (Illus. 2). The spectator tells you of an exchange, giving you the position numbers. Using your thumb and three fingers, keep track of the object originally at Position 2—in this instance, the pencil. For example, Lorna first tells you that she has exchanged the objects at Positions 2 and 3. You move your thumb to finger number 3.

She announces that she has exchanged the objects at Positions 1 and 2. You keep your thumb right where it is, because that's where the pencil remains.

She announces that she has exchanged the objects at Positions 1 and 3.

Illus. 2

Move your thumb to finger number 1, for the pencil now is in Position 1.

You tell Lorna to think of one of the objects and then exchange the other two objects. Then she is to continue exchanging and announcing as in the beginning. You continue to mark the position of the pencil (the original middle object) as though nothing has happened. As you will see, it doesn't matter whether the pencil is actually in that position.

Finally, Lorna is done. You note the number of the finger on which your thumb rests. Turn around and look at the objects. (Remember that Position 1 is on your right, and Position 3 is on your left.) If the pencil is at the same position as the last position marked by your thumb, then the pencil is the selected object. For instance, when Lorna finished, your thumb marked finger number 3; the pencil lies at Position 3. Therefore, the pencil is the chosen object.

But suppose you end up marking finger number 3, and an object other than the pencil is at that position. For example, suppose the key is at Position 3. In this instance, the selected object would be the ring. In the same way, if the ring were at Position 3, the selected object would be the key.

In short: You end up marking finger number 3. If the pencil is at that position, it is the selection. If the pencil is not at that position, it is eliminated. Also eliminated is the object that rests at that position.

Why It Works: You tell Lorna to think of an object and exchange the other two. Suppose that at this point you're marking the pencil as at Position 3. If Lorna decides to think of the pencil, she'll exchange the other two objects—the ring and the key. Lorna once more begins exchanging objects and notifying you of the moves. As she does so, you'll actually continue to mark the position of the pencil. So when she stops, the pencil will be at the position you're marking on your fingers. She must, therefore, have selected the pencil.

Suppose, however, she thinks of the key. The pencil and the ring are exchanged. So in succeeding moves you're marking the position of the ring. At the end, when you see that the ring is at the number you've been marking, you know that the chosen object is not the pencil. Nor can it be the ring, for the ring was exchanged with the pencil. So it must be the key.

In the same way, if the key is at the position you've been marking, you deduce that the choice can't be the pencil or the key; it must be the ring.

The Easy Way

This is essentially an easier version of the previous trick. It can be performed just about anywhere—at your home, at a friend's home, or even in a restaurant. All that is required is three cups and a volunteer who is likely to have a dollar. Linda has a dollar, so get her to help you perform this trick..

Turn the cups upside down and set them side by side. As you're doing this, note the surface of the cups carefully; one of them will probably have a distinguishing mark of some sort. It could be a dot, a slight discoloration, an uneven ridge, whatever (Illus. 3). Note which cup has this mark. Let's suppose that this mark is on the cup to your left; think of this cup as being in Position 1. The cup to the right of this is in Position 2. And the cup to the far right is in Position 3. (If the marked cup were in the center position, you'd think of it as in Position 2; if it were on the right, you'd think of it as in Position 3. This positioning is different from that used in the previous trick where, from your viewpoint, the numbers were reversed so that the spectator could read the numbers from left to right.)

Distinquishing mark

Illus. 3

Say to Linda, "Here we have three cups in a row. In a moment I'll turn my back. When I do, I'd like you to take a dollar bill, crumple it up, and put it under one of the cups. Then exchange the positions of the other two cups. For example, if you put the dollar bill under this cup..." Point to the middle cup. "...then you would exchange the two outside cups." Indicate with your hands how the exchange would be made, but keep the cups in their original order.

Turn away until Linda finishes her task. "The question is, which cup has the dollar under it? I'll choose this one." You turn over the correct cup.

How do you do it? Pretty much the same way as in the previous trick.

All you need do here is figure out which cup has not been moved. Clearly, this will be the correct cup.

In our example, the marked cup is at Position 1. If it's still at that position, then it must have the dollar bill beneath it.

If the marked cup is at Position 2, it means that the cups at Position 1 and Position 2 were exchanged. Therefore, the cup at Position 3 has not been moved and must have the dollar beneath it.

In the same way, if the marked cup is at Position 3, then the cups at

Position 1 and Position 3 have been exchanged. The cup at Position 2 must have remained stationary and must, therefore, be the correct one.

Why It Works: Here is a slightly different way of putting the explanation: When you turn back, you look for the marked cup. If the marked cup is still in the same position (Position 1), it is obviously the correct cup.

Suppose, however, that the marked cup is in Position 2. Then it must have been exchanged with the cup that was in Position 2. This means that the correct cup must be in Position 3.

In the same way, if the marked cup is in Position 3, then it must have been exchanged with the cup at that position. Therefore, the cup at Position 2 has not been moved, so it must be the correct one.

Hummer by Phone

Magicians for years have labored over the Bob Hummer principle used in the two previous tricks. Sam Schwartz came up with a variation which is in many ways the best of the lot. In this version, no object is marked. And the method is puzzling even to those who know the original trick. What's more, the trick may be done over the phone! For clarity and increased interest, I have added a patter theme using three face cards.

All that's required is a deck of cards and a coin (or other small object). So give Marty a phone call, and tell him, with suitable pauses, "Take from the deck a face-card family—a king for the father, a queen for the mother, and a jack for the son. It doesn't matter what the suits are. Place the jack faceup on the table to your left. The jack is in Position 1. Place the queen faceup to the right of the jack; she's in Position 2. And put the king faceup to the right of the queen; he's in position 3.

"You're going to give some money to one of the members of the family—the son, the mother, or the father. So just take a coin and place it on top of one of the three cards, whichever you think is the most deserving.

"Exchange the other two cards. For instance, if you placed the coin on the queen, exchange the jack and king."

You do not ask Marty for any information about this initial move.

"Now, exchange any two cards. Just tell me what positions you're exchanging. For instance, if you're switching the card now at Position 1 with the card at Position 3, just tell me 1 and 3." Marty does this any number of times.

"Now, perform whatever switches you need to bring the family back together in the proper order—jack at Position 1, queen at Position 2, and king at Position 3. As you do this, be sure to tell me what positions you're switching."

Marty finishes. Without asking a question, you tell him on which card the coin rests. You can repeat the stunt any number of times.

It seems absolutely impossible. Yet, your job is quite simple. You start by assuming that the coin is on the card at Position 1. As in "A Sly Inference," you then keep track of this card on your fingers. You hold up the first three fingers of either hand. Mentally number them 1, 2, and 3. To start, place your thumb on the finger designated as 1; this means that, for your purposes, the coin is now at Position 1. Marty tells you of a switch, giving you the position numbers. If the switch involves the card at Position 1, mark the new position on your fingers. Let's say that Marty announces 1 and 3. You move your thumb to the finger designated as 3. The next time Marty switches with the card at 3, you move your thumb to the appropriate finger. (For further explanation, you might read through "A Sly Inference.")

Ultimately, Marty returns the cards to their original positions. And you, of course, continue keeping track of Position 1. Marty announces that he's done. You note which position your thumb is marking. If the thumb is marking Position 1, the card with the coin on it (the jack) is at Position 1. If the thumb is marking the finger designated as 2, the coin lies on the king at Position 3. And, if the thumb rests on the finger designated as 3, the coin lies on the queen at Position 2.

This is important: When your thumb marks finger number 1, the coin is at Position 1. But the other two positions are switched! If your thumb marks number 2, the coin is at Position 3. And if your thumb marks number 3, the coin is at Position 2.

Conclude with some appropriate remark, depending on who received the coin. You might josh Marty about choosing the woman, the queen. Or, if he chooses the jack, you might say, "I suppose you chose the son because he's most in need of money." Or, if he picks the king, you could say, "What makes you think the father needs any more money than he has?"

Why It Works: The basic principle is explained in the "Why It Works" section at the end of "A Sly Inference." Here's the way it works in this instance: Marty places the coin on one of the cards, and then exchanges the other two. You assume that the coin is on the jack, the card at Position 1. You then follow the moves of the card at Position 1. If that card ends up back at Position 1, then the coin must be on it.

Suppose, however, that Marty placed the coin on the queen, the card at Position 2. The other two cards are switched. Therefore, the card originally at Position 3 is now at Position 1, and the card originally at Position 1 is at Position 3. So it is the card that started at Position 3 that you will actually be keeping track of. No matter how many switches are made, eventually the cards are switched back to their original positions. And you'll find that your thumb is marking Position 3. When your thumb marks Position 3, the coin rests on the card at Position 2.

In the same way, if Marty puts the coin on the card at Position 3, the king, the cards at Positions 1 and 2 are exchanged. This puts the card originally at Position 2 at Position 1. And it's the card originally at Position 2 that you'll be keeping track of with your thumb. When Marty says that he's done and that the cards are back in their original order, you'll be marking Position 2 on your fingers. When your thumb marks Position 2, the coin rests on the card at Position 3.

Note: Obviously, cards need not be used in this version; in a pinch, any objects will do.

Getting Along

Here we have a mathematical stunt that purports to be a compatibility test. It's based on an extremely clever card trick.

You'll need the help of a man and a woman, preferably two who are married or friendly.

Let's say that you elicit the aid of Harold and Jan. Explain to them, "I'd like to find out whether you two are really compatible. We'll use numbers in this experiment."

Give each a pad or sheet of paper and a pencil.

"I'd like each of you to jot down a digit—any number from 1 to 9. Now, make sure that neither one of you can see the other person's number."

You, however, have no such restriction. In fact, you make it a point to hand Harold his writing material last. And you hang around long enough to get a glimpse of the digit he jots down. Meanwhile, you're scrupulously careful to keep your head averted so that you can't possibly see Jan's digit. Stroll some distance away, and then have Jan perform the following:

1) Double your number.
2) Add 2.
3) Multiply by 5.

Next, you have Jan subtract a number. The number is actually Harold's number, subtracted from 10. Let's say that Harold chose the number 8. Subtract it from 10, and you get 2. So the next step is:

4) Subtract 2.

Suppose Jan has chosen the number 3 and, as I said, Harold chose 8. Following your instructions, Jan doubles 3, getting 6. She adds 2, getting 8. She multiplies by 5, getting 40. (Harold's number is 8; you've subtracted 8 from 10, getting 2. You tell Jan to subtract 2 from her number.) She subtracts 2, getting 38.

Say to Jan, "You have two digits in your answer, don't you?" She says yes. "What are the digits?" "Three and eight." "And what's the digit you thought of originally?" "Three."

"Three! What a coincidence! One of the digits you came up with is three, and three was your original digit. And, Harold, what's your digit?" "Eight," Harold replies."

"Eight! That was your other digit, Jan. You also came up with Harold's digit! You two are really compatible."

Why It Works: The first three instructions given to Jan automatically produce a two-digit number, the second of which is zero. The first digit is one more than the digit she first chose. Thus, if she chose 1, the number she comes up with is 20. If she chose 2, the number she comes up with is 30. And so on. At this point in the example above, Jan has come up with 40.

You have subtracted Harold's number, 8, from 10. So, in Step 4, you tell Jan to subtract 2 from her total. As you can see, whatever digit is subtracted will produce Jan's original choice as the first digit. And, happily, the subtraction will also produce Harold's choice as the second digit.

Children and Other Pets

Let's try an entertaining trick which can be done for youngsters or oldsters. As you'll see, the person who's assisting you must be a relative stranger. Let's suppose you're performing for a middle-aged man. Turn your back and provide these instructions:

1) Jot down the number of sons you have. (If you have no sons, put down zero.)

2) Multiply by 2. (If you have no sons, the total is still zero.)

3) Add 3.

4) Multiply by 5.

5) Add the number of daughters you have.

6) Multiply by 10.

7) Add the number of pets you have. (Please don't include fish.)

When you're told the total, subtract 150. Chances are, you'll get a three-digit answer. The three digits will indicate the number of sons, the number of daughters, and the number of pets—in that order. So, if your total is 342, the gentleman has 3 sons, 4 daughters, and 2 pets. After considerable concentration, you announce the results.

Suppose your total is 21. This would indicate no sons, 2 daughters, 1 pet.

Suppose the result is 2. This means the man has no children at all, but does have 2 pets.

If the result is 201, the man has 2 sons, no daughters, and 1 pet.

Let's try the trick with a younger person. Turn away and provide these instructions:

1) Jot down the number of brothers you have.

2) Multiply by 2.

3) Add 3.

4) Multiply by 5.

5) Add the number of sisters you have.

6) Multiply by 10.

7) Add the number of pets you have. (Please don't include fish.)

Again, of course, you subtract 150 from the total provided. The first digit of your answer is the number of brothers, the next is the number of sisters, and the third is the number of pets.

Why It Works: This is an example of a "give-and-take" trick. A full explanation is provided at the end of "Birthday Change," pages 10-12, and "More Info," pages 12-14.

CARDS

Playing cards are particularly suited to so-called mathematical tricks. Not only are most of the cards themselves numbered, but also they can be used as objects which can be added to and subtracted from.

I use this shorthand in referring to specific cards: 3H is three of hearts, AS is ace of spades, 9C is nine of clubs, 8D is eight of diamonds, etc.

Five Chosen Cards

This extraordinary trick by Stewart James was shown to me by Milt Kort, undoubtedly with some special techniques by Milt. I modified the ending, which I think makes the trick stronger.

This trick has excellent audience participation, since it requires the assistance of five spectators. Ask one of the spectators to shuffle the deck. You take the deck back and deal a five-card hand to each of your five volunteers. Set the rest of the deck on the table.

"I'd like each of you to mix up your five cards. When you think you've mixed them enough, take a look at your bottom card. Then set your packet of five onto the table. I want you to look at your bottom card, because I wouldn't want you to think I can see your card from the back."

Gather up the five-card packets one on top of the other. Tap the combined packets onto the table as though straightening it out. Actually, you're taking a peek at the bottom card (Illus. 4). Remember its name.

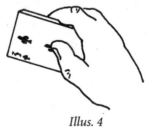

Illus. 4

"I'm going to mix these cards a bit," you tell your audience.

You now perform what I call an "up-and-down shuffle." As you perform the following, each card will be moved beneath the preceding card: Holding the packet in the dealing position, move the top card into your right hand. Move your right hand forward (or upward of the deck) about half its length. Push off the next card, moving it into your right hand. You're now holding two cards in your right hand; the top one extends about half its length above the first card.

Continue going through the packet, the 3rd card going up, the 4th down, and so on. When you are finished, hold the upper group with your left hand as, with your right hand, you strip out the lower group from the others (Illus. 5). This lower group goes on top of the others, and the entire packet is evened up.

"In fact, I'll mix them again."

Perform the up-and-down shuffle again.

Illus. 5

"I'll mix the cards as often as you want," you offer. "Perform the shuffle at least one more time.

When the group indicates that you've shuffled the cards enough, place the packet behind your back. Every fifth card is one of those chosen, and the card you peeked at is still on the bottom.

"I'm going to see if I can find all the chosen cards."

Take four cards off the top of the packet and place them on the bottom. Take the next top card and bring it forward; place it facedown on the table.

Do this twice more.

Now you are ready to find a fourth card. Fan off five cards, retaining their order. Place these on the bottom. This moves one of the chosen cards to the bottom.

Count off five more cards from the top, this time taking them one on top of the other. Replace these on top. This moves the card you peeked at to the top of the deck.

Now, bring the bottom card forward and set it facedown on the table beside the other three. Bring the rest of the packet forward and set it down on top of the rest of the deck, which you set aside earlier.

Turn over one of the four cards. "Whose is this?" A spectator will admit that it's his.

Do the same with the other three cards. Illus. 6 shows the position at this point.

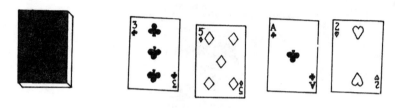

Illus. 6

"There we are. Despite the shuffles, I've located every one of the chosen cards."

A spectator is bound to say something like, "How about my card?"

"Oh, that's right. I haven't located the three of clubs (naming the card you looked at on the bottom)."

Pause a moment to let that sink in. Then tap the top of the deck; turn the top card over. "Ah, here it is!"

Why It Works: Apparently Stewart James figured out this: In a packet of 25 cards, no matter how many up-and-down shuffles you perform, every fifth card will remain at a multiple of five from the top. So, when you complete each up-and-down shuffle, the chosen cards will be at 5th, 10th, 15th, 20th, and 25th positions from the top. The chosen cards will not be at the same positions from the top each time, but they will be at a multiple of 5. The only card which remains at the same position through the shuffles is the card which you peeked at; this stays on the bottom of the packet.

Invisible Deck—Again

Harry A. Canas came up with the basic idea for this trick.

Ask Randy if he will cooperate in an experiment. When he agrees, hand him some paper and a pencil. In fact, take a sheet of paper and a pencil for yourself.

Pretend to remove from your pocket a card case. Open the invisible flap and take out an invisible deck of cards. Say to Randy, "Here I have an ordinary deck of invisible cards." Set the card case down and fan out the invisible deck, the faces toward Randy. "Some people are able to see these cards, Randy. I assume that you can see them all right." Randy can see them just fine. "Please look them over and think of any card that you can see."

When Randy has one in mind, set down the invisible deck, and continue: "While I turn my back, please write down the name of your card on a sheet of paper. When you're done, turn the sheet of paper over."

When he's done, turn back. "Now to make this thoroughly confusing, I'd like someone in the group to name a number from 1 to 25." After the number is named, tell Randy, "Please write that number down."

You also write the number on your sheet of paper. Then you turn away.

Tell Randy, with appropriate pauses, "Put down the value of your card and add it to that first number. Multiply the result by 10. Obviously, your card is either a club, a heart, a spade, or a diamond. So add 1 if your card is a club, 2 if it's a heart, 3 if it's a spade, and 4 if it's a diamond."

When he finishes, get someone in the group to provide a number from 25 to 85. Ask Randy to add that number to his total. You, also, jot that second number on your sheet.

"I'm trying to figure out what your card could possibly be. But I think I'm going to need a hint to help me stimulate my mental powers. What total did you come up with?"

Jot the total he names on your sheet of paper. Apparently you study this as you jot down some figures and concentrate. Actually, you multiply by 10 the first figure provided by the group. (In other words, you put a zero on the end of it.)

Add to this the second figure provided by the group. When Randy gives you his total, you subtract your own total from it. Suppose your final result is 52. The first digit (or digits) tells you the value of the card, so the value is 5. The last digit tells you the suit. As with your instructions, a 1 means clubs, a 2 means hearts, a 3 means spades, and a 4 means diamonds. In this instance, the last digit is 2, so the suit is hearts. The thought-of card is the 5H. Turn back to the group.

After considerable concentration, you pick up the invisible deck, fan through it, and pick out one invisible card. "I think this one is yours, isn't it? The 5H, right?"

Let's try that trick on Betty:

1) She thinks of the 8S, jots it on a sheet, turns the sheet over.

2) Someone in the group names a number from 1 to 25—let's say 18. (You jot this down on a sheet of paper.)

3) Betty also jots down the number, 18, and adds the value of her card to it, giving her 26.

4) She multiplies her total by 10, giving her 260.

5) Betty is told to add 1 for clubs, 2 for hearts, 3 for spades, or 4 for diamonds. (You can remember this order of suits with this mnemonic: CHaSeD—Clubs, Hearts, Spades, Diamonds.) Her card is a spade, so she adds 3, making her total 263.

6) Someone in the group names a number from 25 to 85—let's say 32. (You jot this down on your sheet.)

7) Betty also jots down 32 and adds it to 263, giving her 295.

Betty tells you that her total is 295. Two numbers were provided by the group. The first number was 18. You multiply this by 10, getting 180. You add to this the second chosen number, 32. 180+32=212.

You subtract 212 from Betty's total: 295-212=83. The first digit, 8, gives you the value of Betty's card, and the second digit, 3, indicates that her card is a spade. (Clubs are 1, hearts are 2, spades are 3, diamonds are 4.)

So, she thought of the 8S.

Why It Works: This is another example of a "give-and-take" trick. A full explanation is provided at the end of "Birthday Change," pages 10-12, and "More Info," 12-14.

Unlucky Seven

The basic principle behind Unlucky Seven has been around for a long time, but this particular trick is the invention of George Sands. My only problem was that the original version required 13 cards, which made the trick extremely tedious. My variation, I think, is more effective.

You choose Helene among the multitude of volunteers. Hand her the deck and ask her to give it a good shuffle. As she does so, say, "I don't suppose it will come as any news to you, Helene, that 7 is considered a lucky number. So, I'd like you to count out 7 cards onto the table."

When she finishes, say, "Set the rest of the deck aside. Now, pick out one of those 7 cards. Look at it and show it around."

As she shows the card, pick up the six-card packet in your left hand. "Please hand me your card, Helene." Hold out your right hand to receive the card.

"I'm going to put the packet and your card behind my back. I'm doing this so that you won't know where I'm putting your card in the packet."

Put the cards in your left hand behind your back. At the same time, place the selected card, which is in your right hand, behind your back.

"Let's see. I think I'll put it right there." Actually, place the card on top of the packet.

Bring the packet forward, saying, "In a moment, Helene, you're going to give me a number from 1 to 7. I'll move that number of cards from the top to the bottom of the packet. We'll see what card lies at that number by turning it faceup. We'll use your chosen number again to turn up another card. We'll continue doing this until all the cards are faceup except one. If our minds are in tune and if 7 is really a lucky number, that last card will be the one which you freely chose.

"Now, remember, you freely chose a card, and you'll freely choose a number from 1 to 7. What number do you choose?" If she should happen to say 1, remark, "Not one! Make it a real number."

Chances are overwhelming, however, that she will name some other number. Suppose she chooses the number 4. Counting aloud, move 3 cards from the top to the bottom of the packet, placing them beneath one at a time. As you say four aloud, turn over the fourth card so that all can see it. "Is this your card?" No. Leave this faceup card on top of the packet. It becomes the first card moved to the bottom in the next count.

Repeat the procedure, moving 3 cards to the bottom of the packet and turning the fourth card faceup. Leave this card faceup on top of the packet. As before, this becomes the first card moved to the bottom in the next count.

Fan through the cards from time to time so that you'll know when only one card remains facedown. Continue the counting procedure until only one card remains facedown. Fan through the cards, showing that only one is still facedown. Turn over the chosen card. "And there it is, your card. The last one remaining facedown."

If the group insists, you may repeat the trick.

Why It Works: The trick works with any prime number of cards and with any selected number that is not higher than the number of cards. (The number 1, obviously, will not work.) What is a prime number? Well, no number will divide evenly into it, except the number 1 or the prime number itself. In other words, if you divide anything into it, you always have a remainder. Prime numbers up to 20 are 1, 3, 5, 7, 11, 13, 17, 19.

How in the world could anyone discover the basic principle involved in this trick? I don't know. But I think it may have been serendipity—a happy accident. Someone was fooling around with a deck of cards one day and wondered, "What if..." That's the way I've invented many of my tricks.

Two Are Better Than One

Two old tricks were cleverly combined by George Kaplan to produce a real winner. In this instance, you'll be using playing cards, but you could also use coins, dominoes, whatever.

You'll need two persons to assist you. Jack and Mary are kind enough to volunteer. Hand Jack a deck of cards, saying, "I'd like you to deal out a row of cards facedown, one right next to the other. You can deal whatever number of cards you wish. But I don't want anyone else to know how many cards you're using. So would you go to one side so no one can see? " Or, if it's convenient, he could step into the next room. "Please tell me when you're done."

When he's ready, continue: "Jack, please deal another row of cards just below that first row. But put one less card in that row. For instance, if you had 10 cards in your top row, put 9 cards in your bottom row."

Let's say that Jack chooses to deal out 7 cards as his top row and 6 in his bottom row.

$$1 \quad 2 \quad 3 \quad 4 \quad 5 \quad 6 \quad 7$$
$$1 \quad 2 \quad 3 \quad 4 \quad 5 \quad 6$$

When he's done, say, "Now please name any number that's less than the number of cards in your bottom row."

Let's say he names 3. You remember it.

"Take that many cards away from the top row and set them aside."

This leaves 4 cards in the top line.

$$1 \quad 2 \quad 3 \quad 4$$
$$1 \quad 2 \quad 3 \quad 4 \quad 5 \quad 6$$

"Whatever number of cards you now have in the top line, take away from the bottom line. Set them aside, also."

Jack takes 4 cards from the bottom line, leaving 2.

$$1 \quad 2 \quad 3 \quad 4$$
$$1 \quad 2$$

"Remove the rest of the cards from the top line and set them aside."

$$1 \quad 2$$

Jack has 2 cards left. "We've gone through all this, Jack, to make sure you end up with a random number. Now, don't tell anyone how many cards you have left."

But, of course, you know how many he has left. He has one less than the number he named. He named the number 3, so the number of cards he has left is 2.

Turn to Mary. You'll now force the number 2 on her. Give her these directions, with appropriate pauses: "Mary, please think of any number from 1 to 10. Double it. Add 2. Multiply by 5."

At this point, you mentally subtract Jack's number from 10. His number is 2, so you subtract 2 from 10, getting 8. Tell Mary to subtract this number, 8, from her total.

"Now, let's see if coincidence will operate. Mary, you probably have a number with two digits in it, right?" Right. "We don't care about the first digit; what's the second one?"

It's 2.

"Jack, what number of cards did you end up with?"

He ended up with 2.

"Unbelievable! You both had 2. You guys are terrific; you should definitely be a team."

Why It Works: Although the first part of this trick may appear to be, in some way, mathematical, it is primarily verbal. Let's assume that you're the spectator and that you're told to deal out two rows of cards, both rows containing the same number of cards.

> 1 2 3 4 5 6
> 1 2 3 4 5 6

You choose a number—4, let's say. You remove that number of cards from the top row.

> 1 2
> 1 2 3 4 5 6

Now, remove from the bottom line the same number of cards as you have remaining in the top line.

> 1 2
> 1 2 3 4

Remove the rest of the top line, and you're left with four cards. It is not so mysterious, is it? Since both rows have the same number of cards in them, you can see that whatever number you remove from the top line will be what's eventually left in the bottom line. The only difference is this: With one more card in the top line, you'll subtract one more from the bottom line. Thus, the bottom line will be one less than the chosen number.

In effect, you're given these instructions:

1) Deal out a row of any number of cards. (You deal 8.)

2) Think of any number that's less than the number of cards in that row. (You think of the number 5.)

3) Mentally subtract that number from your total number of cards. (8-5=3.)

4) Remove that number of cards from your row. (You do: 8-3=5.)

5) Oh, and by the way, take away another card. (You do: 5-1=4.)

Can you believe it! You ended up with one less than your chosen number.

The second part of this trick is the familiar "give-and-take" routine. See the Why It Works sections in "Birthday Change" and "More Info" on pages 10-14.

Double-Surprise

When I first saw this trick, I thought it was clever but tedious. I eliminated some nonessential parts, added some convincing touches, and tossed in patter to make the weaker points seem logical. The result: a trick which interests audiences and which I enjoy doing.

To begin, you'll need a setup. In the original version, this was done in advance. I prefer to do it with the audience present, thus making the trick completely impromptu. Say, "I'll try to get one card of each value, so that I can offer a good variety to choose from."

For purposes of your setup, you must consider every spot card to have its face value. For the face cards, the jack will have a value of 11, the queen 12, and the king 13. The ace is counted as 1.

Fan through the deck, the faces of the cards toward yourself. Remove any 3 and place it facedown onto the table. On top of this, place a card which is 3 values higher than the 3. What's 3 more than the 3? Obviously, 6. So remove any 6 and place it facedown on top of the 3. Remove any 9 (3 more than 6) and place it facedown on the pile.

What's 3 more than 9? 12. A queen has a value of 12. So remove any queen and place it facedown on top of the 9.

But what is 3 more than the queen? You count the king as 1, and then you start at the beginning of a 1-to-13 sequence. So the ace would be counted as 2, and the third card in the count would be a 2. So you place a 2 facedown on top of the pile.

Continue adding a card that is 3 more than the previous one. The last card you'll deal on top of the pile will be a king. Here's the entire sequence from top to bottom. (Note that it's the reverse of the order in which the cards are placed down.)

K 10 7 4 A J 8 5 2 Q 9 6 3

While making this setup, you should mutter comments like, "Oh, yes, I'll need one of those," and, "Sure, how could we do this without a 7?"

(If you prefer, you may simply have your setup on top before you begin. Set the cards up as described above. Then place the stack on top of the deck. Start the trick by fanning off 13 cards from the top and taking them from the deck. The person who showed me the original trick started like this; I don't see any advantage to it, however.)

In either instance, you set the rest of the deck aside, for it won't be used during the remainder of the trick.

Get things started by asking Justine to give the 13-card packet a complete cut. (As you'll see, this business of having the cards cut will become a sort of running gag.)

Fan the faces of the cards so that all the spectators can see the values. But only allow a casual look—a few seconds should be enough. "They seem pretty well mixed," you say. "But we'd better cut them."

Again, ask Justine to give the packet a complete cut. You pick up the packet, saying, "Besides that, I'd better give them a good mix."

You now perform the same up-and-down shuffle described in "Five Chosen Cards," pages 26-28. You start by pushing the top card up, the next one down, and so on. When you finish, strip out the lower portion and place it on top.

Hold the cards up, and spread them out so that only the spectators can see the faces (Illus. 7). This time, give the group plenty of time to look them over "I imagine they're pretty well mixed by now, but..." Close the cards up and set the packet on the table. "...maybe we'd better cut them." Have Justine cut the packet again. "And, I'd better mix them some more."

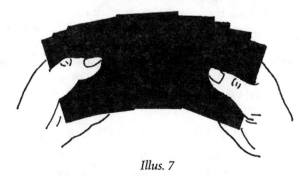

Illus. 7

Close the cards up and repeat the "up-and-down shuffle." Again, strip out the cards you've pushed down and place these on top of the others.

"You know what?" By this time, the spectators should have the idea. "Maybe we'd better cut them."

Ask Justine to give the packet another cut. "And I'd also like you to select a card, Justine. Then look at it and show it around." Spread the packet facedown between your hands and have her select a card. As she looks at the card and shows it to others, separate the packet at the point from which the card was taken. Place the cards in your right hand below those in your left hand. In other words, cut the packet at the point from which the card was taken. Respread the packet and have Justine push her card in wherever she wishes.

Close up the cards and say, "You know what, Justine?" She probably does. No matter. You still say, "Maybe we'd better cut them." Justine gives the packet at least two complete cuts.

"I'll now use my special power to see if I can locate your card." In this instance, your special power consists of the ability to tell what card is not in its proper place in a sequence.

Your second "up-and-down shuffle" arranged the cards so that they ran in sequence from ace to king. It's unlikely that the top card was an ace and the bottom card a king, but the sequence is still there, regardless of the number of cuts. So the sequence might begin with the ace in the middle and work down to the 7 as the bottom card. The 8, then, would be the top card, continuing the sequence. And the one below that would be the 9, and so on.

A typical sequence, from the top down, might be:

5 6 7 8 9 10 J Q K A 2 3 4

You can see, then, that when Justine chose a card and you cut at the point where she took the card, she must return the card so that it's out of sequence. The exception would be if she returned the card to the top or bottom of the packet; I've never had this happen.

So you simply hold the packet, faces toward yourself, fan through the cards and find the one that's out of sequence. But before you do this, cut the packet so that the ace becomes the top card. Now look through the packet. This might be the arrangement:

A 2 3 4 6 7 8 9 10 J 5 Q K

Obviously, the 5 is the card which is out of sequence. Remove this card and place it facedown on the table. Close up the remaining cards and hold them in your left hand in the dealer's grip. Ask Justine to name her card. She names it. You then indicate that she should turn the card faceup.

This is miracle number 1. How could you possibly have found her card? Nod your head. Mutter, "Very good." Apparently the trick is over.

But as she was turning her card over, you casually fanned down to where the chosen card could be placed in proper sequence. In our example, the card is a 5, so you spread four cards to the right. Hold the cards in your left hand as shown in Illus. 8. After the selected card is shown around, take it in your right hand, and put it facedown fifth from the top. Close up the cards and casually set them facedown onto the table.

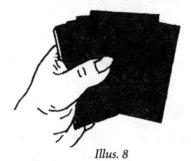

Illus. 8

At this point you'd like to distract the spectators for a few moments, providing "time misdirection." You say to Justine, "Notice that you chose whatever card you wished and placed it back wherever you wished. Furthermore, the cards were cut...a few times."

That should be long enough. "Now let's see what happens when I give these a riffle?" Pick up the packet and riffle the ends. Deal them out face-up from right to left, overlapping as you go. This enables the spectators to see all the values right-side up (Illus. 9). The cards are, of course, in order from A to K. And that's miracle number 2.

Illus. 9

Why It Works: The idea is that you want to end up with the cards in sequence from A to K. Clearly, you must work backwards. So you start with this sequence (from top to bottom):

A 2 3 4 5 6 7 8 9 10 J Q K

In the last move of the up-and-down shuffle, a group of 6 cards is placed on top. Prior to this move, these would be every second card in the packet:

_ A _ 2 _ 3 _ 4 _ 5 _ 6 _

The rest, obviously, would be the bottom 7 cards, and they would fit in like this:

<u>7</u> A <u>8</u> 2 <u>9</u> 3 <u>10</u> 4 J 5 Q 6 <u>K</u>

Since you want to perform two up-and-down shuffles, you must move back another step. Again, the top 6 cards would become every second card:

_ 7 _ A _ 8 _ 2 _ 9 _ 3 _

And, once more, the bottom 7 cards would fit in like this:

<u>10</u> 7 <u>4</u> A J 8 <u>5</u> 2 Q 9 <u>6</u> 3 <u>K</u>

So this is the order which, with two up-and-down shuffles, will produce the A to K order. (You'll note that this is slightly different from the order in which I had you set the cards up at the beginning—the king is on the bottom rather than on top. Since the packet is cut repeatedly without changing the basic order, this is irrelevant.)

Note: In many tricks, I like to throw in a running gag. This helps keep the group interested. In this one, it's the business of cutting the cards. How did this occur to me? A gentleman showed me the basic trick and explained it. As I started working it, I decided to cut the cards. He said, "Oh, no, don't do that." Pause. "Oh, I guess it would be all right." Being a somewhat perverse person, it occurred to me at that moment that it might be fun to have the cards cut repeatedly.

Simple Miraskill

My guess is that Stewart James's marvelous trick, Miraskill, has had dozens of variations. I came up with a pretty good one myself a few years ago. Recently I developed a much simpler version, one which requires no great skill, yet retains the strong impact of the original effect. No sleights are involved, and it's very direct.

I was very proud of my invention until recently, when someone pointed out to me that some sneak had previously invented the same basic idea.

Grace is superb at following directions, so she'd be the perfect choice to assist you with this experiment.

Start by fanning through the cards from the top of the deck, muttering, "Let's see, we'll need about half the deck." Actually, you're mentally counting the cards in groups of three, intending to stop after you have exactly 24 cards fanned into your right hand.

At this point, separate your hands. Eyeing the cards in each hand, you say, "That's close enough." The cards in your right hand are turned faceup. Now perform a riffle shuffle, the 28 facedown cards in your left hand being intermixed with the 24 faceup cards in your right hand. Then perform a few overhand shuffles and another riffle shuffle. (If you can't do a riffle shuffle, simply place the facedown group in your left hand on top of the faceup group in the your hand. Perform a number of overhand shuffles.)

Hand the deck to Grace. "Please give the cards a good shuffle, Grace." She does. "And another one, if you wish."

When she's done, say, "I'm about to make a prediction, but I'll need some help." Point to the deck. "Hand me a card, please."

Take the card and hold it, face outward, against your forehead (Illus. 10). Ask a question about the card, something like, "Is that a black card?" Whatever the answer, say, "Okay. I have my prediction." Return the card to the deck. If it were originally faceup, make sure it's still faceup; and if it were facedown, make sure it's still facedown.

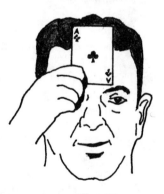

Illus. 10

"Please shuffle the cards again, Grace."

When she finishes, make your prediction. Either write it on a sheet of paper, or make it aloud. If you make it aloud, repeat it at least once. (Stating your prediction aloud actually works pretty well, especially when it's impossible to write the prediction down. Whispering it to a spectator is not a great idea; others suspect that you're using a confederate.) Your prediction: "Four more facedown cards than faceup cards."

Tell Grace, "Spread out the top two cards. If they're both faceup, put them in a pile to the right. If they're both facedown, put them in a pile to the left. If one is faceup and one facedown, put them in a pile in the middle. Continue doing this through the entire deck."

Guide her as she does this. When she finishes, have her count the face-down pile, and have another spectator count the faceup pile. Each announces the total. You repeat the result. For instance: "16 facedown cards, and 12 faceup cards. So there are four more facedown cards." Have your prediction read.

"Let's try that again. Grace, please hand me one of your cards." She hands you one of her facedown cards. You hold the card up to your forehead, face outward. Again, you ask a question, like "What color is it?" or "Is it a face card?"

Whatever the answer, turn the card over and look at it. Say, "Good, now I know my prediction." Immediately look around for your pencil and paper. As you do so, casually drop the card you're holding faceup onto the middle pile. Place the other two piles on top and then give the deck a little shuffle. At this point the deck consists of 27 facedown cards and 25 faceup cards. Hand the deck to Grace and ask her to shuffle. When she finishes, you make your next prediction: "Two more facedown cards."

Grace forms three piles as before. The face-down pile is counted by Grace, the faceup pile by another spectator. Your prediction is correct again.

Once more, ask Grace to hand you one of her cards. Place the card to your forehead, ask the stupid question, drop the card faceup onto the middle pile. Collect the cards. You're now holding 26 faceup cards mixed in with 26 facedown cards. Give the cards a little shuffle, hand them to Grace, and ask her to shuffle them. Your prediction this time: The two piles are equal.

Again, your prediction turns out to be absolutely accurate.

Why It Works: Here is what Stewart James discovered. Go through a deck one pair at a time, noting the colors involved in each pair. There are three possibilities: Both cards are red, both are black, or one card is red and the other black. When they are divided into three piles, the mixed pile will vary in size, but the red pile and the black pile will always have an equal number of cards. I assume that James then speculated, "What if I remove a certain number of cards of one color?" When he removed four red cards and went through the indicated procedure, the black pile contained four more cards than the red pile. When he removed two red cards and went through the indicated procedure, the black pile contained two more cards than the red pile. So he developed this into a prediction trick.

When all this is explained, you might wonder, "When the black pile contains four more cards than the red pile, isn't it obvious that four red cards are missing from the deck? After all, the middle pile always contains an equal number of reds and blacks. There should be an equal number of cards in each of the other two piles."

I performed the original trick for years, and absolutely no one was ever logical enough to figure out the solution.

I think there are two advantages to my version: 1) You don't subtract cards from the deck, nor do you add cards. 2) Since you're working with faceup and facedown cards and no one is aware of how many you have of each, the basic principle is even better disguised.

Note: There's a reason that you don't make your prediction until the spectator finishes shuffling. The combination of faceup and facedown cards might confuse the spectator. In the process of shuffling, she might turn the deck over. No problem. Just watch carefully. If she does turn the deck over, reverse your prediction. For instance, you intended to write down, "Four more facedown cards." Now you'll write, "Four more faceup cards."

DICE

When I do tricks with the numbers on dice, I find it advisable to provide some sort of rationale. For instance, I might say, "Sometimes I seem to have an affinity for the numbers on the dice. But not always. Frequently it works, however, when various numbers on the dice are manipulated. Let me show you what I mean."

It shouldn't be too difficult for you to develop patter similar, but superior, to the above. You'll find some additional patter ideas below.

The Dice Are Cast

Dan is probably proficient at counting dots, so ask him to help you out. Hand him two dice, saying, "I'd like to attempt an experiment with these dice. I'm going to turn my back and have you roll the dice. Then I'll try to figure out what numbers you rolled."

You turn away, and Dan rolls the dice. "I can't seem to get the numbers. I'll need some connection, however remote, to the numbers on the dice. Consider one of the dice as Die 1. Look at the number showing on that die. Double that number. Add 1 to that. Multiply the result by 5.

"Look at the number showing on Die 2. Add that to your total. Please remember that total.

"Now take Die 1 into your left hand and Die 2 into your right hand."

Turn back to the group. "So, Dan, what total did you come up with?"

He tells you the total. "Please hand me Die 1." He does; you examine the die and tell him what number he rolled with it.

You ask Dan for Die 2. Again, you examine the die and tell the number that was rolled with it.

Difficult? Not in the least. When Dan tells you his total, you subtract 5. If, for instance, Dan says his total is 57, you subtract 5, getting 52. The first digit tells you what Dan had on Die Number 1; the second digit tells you what he had on Die 2. So Dan rolled a 5 and a 2.

Suppose Dan tells you his total is 39. You subtract 5, getting 34. Die Number 1 was a 3, and Die Number 2 was a 4.

Dan gives you a total of 21. You subtract 5, getting 16. Die 1 was a 1, and Die 2 was a 6.

Review:

1) Roll the dice. Number them 1 and 2.
2) Double the number showing on Die 1, add 1, multiply by 5.

42

3) Add to the total the number showing on Die 2.

4) You subtract 5 from the total. The first digit gives you the total on Die 1; the second gives you the total on Die 2.

Why It Works: Although it's not readily apparent, this is another application of the "give-and-take" idea first discussed in "Birthday Change," pages 10-12, and expanded on in "More Info," pages 12-14.

There are several possibilities, but here's one way you might work out the trick. Assume that the spectator has rolled numbers 3 and 4, and that he has decided to designate 3 as Die 1 and 4 as Die 2. So you want a way where you can end up with the number 34.

Now, start working backwards. You want to make the trick relatively easy, like getting the number by just subtracting 5. So add 5 to 34, getting 39.

How can you work it so that the spectator gets to 39? Again, there are many options, but let's take the path probably pursued by the inventor of this trick. As the last operation, why not have the spectator add on the value of Die 2? We have 39, so we subtract 4. That gives us 35.

How can you now use the value on Die 1 to arrive at 35? Clearly, not just anything will work. Considerable experimentation is necessary. One way that works—and the eventual choice of the inventor of the trick—is to double the number, add 1, and multiply by 5.

You get the same result by multiplying Die 1 by 10 and adding 5. But if you work it out that way, it gets a little too obvious.

You might work out a different way yourself.

Have a Roll

Here we have a trick that's similar to the previous trick. Since this trick uses three dice, it's half again better than the other.

Let's use Linda this time. Give her three dice, saying, "When my back is turned, Linda, please roll these three dice."

Turn away. After she rolls the dice, provide these directions:

1) Multiply the number on Die 1 by 2.

2) Add 5.

3) Multiply by 5.

4) Note the number on Die 2. Add this to the total.

5) Multiply by 10.

6) Note the number on Die 3. Add this to the total.

Take your time, to make sure that she gets the instructions right. Finally, say, "What total did you get, Linda?" She gives you her total.

After pondering this information, you reveal what number is showing on each die.

You're able to accomplish this magnificent result by subtracting 250 from her number. Suppose she tells you her answer is 612. 612-250=362.

So the numbers showing on the dice are 3, 6, and 2.

It's just possible that the subtraction might be a bit challenging for an offhand demonstration. There's nothing wrong with doing the math on a sheet of paper, and then putting the paper away after you're done. As you jot down the numbers, you might say, "My mind is barraged by numbers. I can't seem to distinguish which ones are on your dice."

Why It Works: The same explanation as given for the previous trick, "The Dice Are Cast," applies here. You might find it interesting to work backwards, using the same technique as I describe there.

Take Two

Once more I'm indebted to that legendary master of close-up magic, Milt Kort, who showed me the next two tricks. He mentioned that they were not original with him.

Hugo, always a good sport, volunteers to assist you in a mental experiment. Hand him two dice, turn your back, and tell him, "Hugo, I'd like you to roll those dice. Then pick them up and roll them again. Continue on. When you're satisfied with the two numbers you've rolled, tell me."

Hugo is finally satisfied with his numbers.

"Add together the two numbers that are showing, but don't tell me the result." Hugo obliges. "Turn one of the dice completely over. Add that number to your total." Hugo does so.

"Take that same die and roll it. Whatever number comes up—add that to your total."

You turn around. "Please concentrate on your total, Hugo." You, too, concentrate. Actually, you glance at the dice and immediately name the total Hugo is thinking of.

How? Simply add the numbers showing on the dice, and then add 7. Suppose that one die shows 5 and the other 4. You add these together, getting 9. You add 7 to 9, getting 16, which is Hugo's total.

Why It Works: The opposite sides of a die always total 7. Many persons know this, so it's up to the clever magician to disguise this principle. Let's review what actually happens:

The dice are rolled onto the table and totaled. (Let's say that Die A shows 5 and Die B shows 3.) Through the rest of the trick, Die A will not be changed at all; it simply remains on the table.

Die B is turned over and its other side is added to the total. Since opposite sides of a die always total 7, Hugo has added 7 to the total shown on Die A: 7+5=12.

He rolls Die B again. Let's say that the number 4 comes up. He adds 4 to the 12, getting 16. Die A still shows 5, and Die B now shows 4. The only amount missing is the total of the two sides of Die B, 7. When you turn around, add this missing 7 to the total of the other two dice: 7+5+4=16.

Talk 'n' Roll

Here you have an excellent follow-up to the preceding trick. Hugo and the rest of the group ask you to perform the trick again. You know better than that. Besides, you have a variation which is even more mystifying.

"Let's make it more difficult," you say. Toss a third die onto the table. Turn your back. "Hugo, I'd like you to roll all three of the dice until you get three numbers that you like." He does it.

"Please add together the top numbers."

(At this point, you might want to call in Harriet to work with Hugo. Addition may not be his specialty.)

"Turn two of the dice over. Add these two numbers to your total."

When Hugo finishes, continue: "Pick up either one of these two dice and put it into your pocket. Done? Now, take the other one of those two and roll it. Add the top number to your total."

Turn around, glance at the two dice on the table, and tell Hugo his total. Incredible! You see only two of the dice involved.

How? Just add the total of the two dice, and add 14.

Why It Works: Once more, the opposite sides of a die total 7. So, let's examine what really happens.

Hugo tosses the three dice and adds them up. Let's say that Die A is 3; it will stay just as it is through the rest of the trick. The two other dice are turned over and are added in. Opposite sides of a die total 7. Therefore, Die B and Die C have thus far totaled 7+7, or 14.

Putting one of the two dice in your pocket doesn't change anything; the total of the two is still 14. So, presently, the total is 3 for Die A, plus 14, the total established for Die B and Die C.

Let's say that Hugo has put Die B into his pocket. He rolls Die C another time, and its number is added to the total. Let's say that the number is 6. So the correct total is easily obtained by adding Die A (3) to Die C (6),both of which are showing, and then adding 14, the total of the two sides of Die B and Die C after the initial throw. So, the total is 3+6+14=23.

MIND READING

When presenting certain mental tricks, why are you using numbers? It's best to have some sort of explanation. Here are several thoughts, some of which you may decide to use in your patter.

"In our daily lives, numbers surround us from the time we get up until we go to bed. It's six o'clock—time to get up. How many pieces of toast will I have for breakfast? I take I-75 to work. I take the elevator to the 3rd floor. My office is 345. I got caught in traffic, and I was 5 minutes late. On and on. We are constantly working with numbers. This practice makes it easier to make certain associations when performing feats of mentalism using numbers.

"Furthermore, through the ages, certain numbers were considered to have mystical qualities. We all know that 7 is considered lucky, and 13 is considered unlucky. We've heard the expression 'Good things come in 3's.' It doesn't matter if any of this is true. Mentalism is extremely difficult, so the mentalist has to take advantage of any possibility, however remote. The idea in using numbers is this: It might help; it couldn't hurt.

"Digits, like individual letters of the alphabet, are easy to visualize. If telepathy works, this would simplify the operation. It's also helpful that the digits do not look at all alike. Yes, it's possible sometimes to confuse a 3 with an 8 or a 6 with a 9, but no others could possibly get confused. So, for thought transference, digits are ideal."

Working Together

Raymond is good at multiplication, so he'll be your perfect assistant. "I'm going to try to read your mind, Raymond. We must work together for this to operate."

Turn your back.

"Please write down any four-digit number. Now, together, we'll multiply this by some two-digit number. You choose one digit; I'll choose the other. What do you choose?" Whatever he chooses, you choose a digit which will add up to 9 with the digit he has chosen.. He chooses 6; you choose 3. He chooses 9; you choose zero. "Now, using these two digits in any order, multiply your four- digit number."

Make sure he understands. Let's suppose he has written down this four- digit number: 9836.

He has chosen the digit 4. You have chosen 5 (9-4=5). He puts the digits in either order. Let's say he chooses 54. He multiplies his 4-digit number by this:

$$
\begin{array}{r}
9836 \\
\times 54 \\
\hline
39344 \\
49180 \\
\hline
531144
\end{array}
$$

"Raymond, circle one of the digits in your answer. But please don't circle zero because, after all, zero is really nothing. You may not have noticed, but that's a small joke—almost as small as zero.

"Have you circled one of the digits? Good. I'm going to try to read your mind and name that digit that you've circled. But I'll need help. Very slowly, tell me what the other digits are in your answer. You can tell me in any order, but be sure to name all of them—even the duplicates."

As Raymond names the digits, you add them together. When he is done, reduce the total to a single digit. For instance, Raymond names these digits: 5, 1, 4, 3, 1. As he does so, you add them up. In this instance, you end up with 14. You add together the 1 and the 4, getting 5. Once you have the single digit, you subtract it from 9; this gives you the circled digit. Here, you have 5, so you subtract it from 9, getting 4. That would be the digit that Raymond circled.

Suppose Raymond circled the 3. In some order he would name the other digits: 5, 1, 1, 4, 4. As he names them, you add them together. The result is 15. You add together the 1 and 5, getting 6. Subtract the 6 from 9 and you get the circled digit, 3.

The trick may be repeated.

If the spectator's digits reduce to 9, his circled digit is also a 9.

Why It Works: You'll find information about some of the strange properties of the number 9 at the end of the trick "Of an Age," on pages 7-9. It's pointed out there that any number multiplied by 9 will produce an answer which will reduce to the number 9. For example: 856×9=7704.

Reduce the digits in the answer to a single digit. 7+7+0+4=18.

Reduce the 18 to a single digit. 1+8=9.

Even more peculiar is this: If either number in a multiplication problem can be reduced to 9, the product can also be reduced to 9. It doesn't matter how long the numbers are. For instance, you might multiply 9846238 (which reduces to 4) by 75231 (which reduces to 9). You just might want to try this out on your calculator.

If you'll take my word for it, the answer is 740,742,330,978. Add up those digits and you get 54. Add the 5 and 4 and you get—9!

In this trick, you make sure that the multiplier can be reduced to 9 by inserting a digit that will add up to 9 with the spectator's digit. Therefore, the answer can be reduced to 9. Obviously, the circled number is easily determined by subtracting the reduced total of the other numbers from 9.

And the Number Is ...

Since you clearly possess astonishing powers of extrasensory perception, it is understandable that you should point this out to the group before presenting this conclusive demonstration.

Rosemary can balance her checkbook, so get her to assist you. "Rosemary, I want you to arrive at a random number, and then we'll see whether I can discern what it is." Turn away, and then proceed with these instructions: "Write down a number with five digits in it."

Suppose she writes down 69254 (Illus. 11).

Illus. 11

"Now, add up the digits in your number, and write the result on one side."

If she has trouble understanding this, explain, "If your number were 22222, you would add up the five twos, giving you 10."

Rosemary adds the digits in 69254 and gets 26, which she writes to one side (Illus. 12).

"Circle any digit you want in your original number. We'll not be using that digit right now."

Let's say that Rosemary circles the 2 (Illus. 13).

"Write the rest of the number above the number you put down to one side. So you'll be writing a four-digit number above the number you wrote to one side" (Illus. 14).

"Now, subtract the smaller number from the larger number" (Illus. 15).

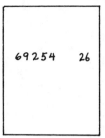

Illus. 12

Illus. 13

Illus. 14

"I have no way of knowing any of your original numbers. But to make the proper mental association, I would like to know your final number."

Rosemary tells you that it's 6928.

"Concentrate, please, on the number you circled." Pause, brow wrinkled in thought. "The number is two."

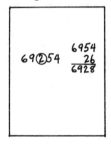

Illus. 15

You can repeat the stunt if you wish—several times.

To get the correct answer, you reduce the number given to you by the spectator to a single digit and subtract it from nine. In the example, you were given 6928. 6+9+2+8=25. 2+5=7. (Most of the time, the calculation isn't even this complicated.) Now, subtract the result from nine, and you have the spectator's circled number. In this instance, you subtract 7 from 9, getting 2.

Let's try another example. The spectator jots down a five-digit number: 85731. She adds the digits, getting 24. She jots 24 to one side.

She circles one of the digits in the original number. Let's say she circles the 8. This leaves her with 5731. She writes this above the number she wrote to one side and subtracts:5731-24=5707.

She tells you the result, which is 5707. You mentally add the digits: 5+7+0+7=19. You must reduce this to a single digit, so you add 1 and 9, getting 10. Still two digits, so: 1+0=1. You subtract 1 from 9, and you get the value of the circled digit,8.

Why It Works: Once more, it's the power of 9. After I explain, I'll bet you can come up with a trick way better than the one I just described.

Take any number and add the digits. Subtract the result from the original number. When you reduce the answer to a single digit, guess what—the result is 9.

So a 5-digit number is written down. The digits are added up and the result is set down to one side. If you subtract this result from the 5-digit number, you'll get 9. Instead, circle one of the digits in the 5-digit number, leaving you with a 4-digit number. You subtract your reduced number from the 4-digit number. You reduce the answer and get a single digit which, when subtracted from 9, gives you the value of the circled number.

This point might be of interest. As I mentioned, you can take any number and add the digits. When you subtract this total from the original number, you get a number that can be reduced to 9. You can also take any number, add the digits, reduce these digits to a single digit, and subtract this single digit from the original number. Once again, the answer can be reduced to 9.

A Good Call

This item is quite similar to the previous trick. What makes it different is the use of a telephone and a medium.

Since you're pretty sure that Don knows how to operate a telephone, you might as well solicit his aid. "Don, in a moment you're going to make a phone call to Madame Anastasia, who will try to read your mind. But first, I'd like you to write down the last four digits of any phone number you wish."

Let's say that Don jots down 7082.

"Please add the digits together."

He adds them: 7+0+8+2=17.

"Now please subtract that answer from your original number."

Don subtracts 17 from 7082, getting 7065.

"Please circle one of the digits. This will be your selected number."

Let's say that Don circles the number 6. You then provide him with a phone number and ask him to call and ask for Madame Anastasia. When Don phones, he is either connected directly with Madame Anastasia or she is called to the phone. She immediately says to Don, "What are the three digits you did not choose?"

Don tells her, "Seven, zero, five."

Madame Anastasia tells him that his chosen number is 6.

How does she know? Why, she simply adds together the three digits she is provided and then—if need be—she reduces the total to a single digit: 7+0+5=12, and then 1+2=3.

She subtracts the result from 9: 9-3=6.

Madame Anastasia is advised in advance that you're going to perform the trick and is told the secret.

Let's try another example. The phone number is 1425. The spectator adds these together: 1+4+2+5=12.

He subtracts 12 from 1425, getting 1413.

The spectator circles the number 4, calls your confederate, and lists the other three digits: 1, 1, 3. Your confederate adds them up, getting 5. She subtracts 5 from 9, getting 4, the chosen number.

As with the previous trick, if the spectator's digits reduce to 9, her circled digit is also a 9.

Why It Works: The explanation at the end of the previous trick, "And the Number Is ...," tells you all you need to know. Add the digits of any number and subtract the total from the original number. You end up with a number which can be reduced to 9.

A Little Help

Mary Jane has been an attentive spectator; the very least you can do is read her mind for her. Turn your back and provide these instructions:

1) Jot down a single digit.(She jots down 7.)
2) Put a zero after it.(She makes it 70.)
3) Add the original digit to your number.(7+70=77.)
4) Multiply by 3.(3×77=231.)
5) Multiply by 11. (11×231=2541.)
6) Multiply by 3. (3×2541=7623.)

"Mary Jane, I've tried to make sure that you've chosen a number completely at random. I'll now read your mind and reveal that number." You concentrate fiercely, but it's no use. "I seem to see a 5...no...I'm not sure. I can't seem to get the number. Perhaps if you provide a little help. What's the last digit?"

Since her number is 7623, she tells you that it's 3.

You know that the answer is always a four-digit number. You will now generate the digits in order, from first to last, so that you can read Mary Jane's mind gradually...but not too gradually.

Mary Jane told you that the last digit is 3.

To determine the first digit, subtract the last digit from 10: 10-3=7.

"I see the number 7. Yes, 7 is the first digit."

To determine the second digit, subtract 1 from the first digit: 7-1=6.

"And...let's see...the second digit is 6."

To determine the third digit, subtract 1 from the last digit: 3-1=2.

"The third digit...Oh, yes, that's a 2."

Pause. "And, as you mentioned, the last digit is 3. So your number is 7623."

Another example: You ask the spectator what the last digit is. She tells you that it's 7.

Subtract 7 from 10, getting 3.

Subtract 1 from 3, getting 2. 32.

Subtract 1 from 7, the number you were given, getting 6. 326.

Throw in the 7. 3267.

If the spectator's digits reduce to 9, the chosen number is also a 9.

Why It Works: Here we have yet another example of a "give-and-take" trick. A full explanation is provided at the end of "Birthday Change," pages 10-12 , and "More Info," pages 12-14.

It's quite apparent that the person who created this trick had to do quite a bit of experimenting before ending up with a procedure that would bring about the desired results.

Note: Suppose you decide to repeat the trick. After the spectator finishes the arithmetic, you might say, "I can't seem to get the answer. Would you please give me any one of the digits."

After you're given the digit, say, "I can't seem to visualize which digit you gave me. Is it the first, second, third, or fourth?"

Obviously, when you're told which one it is, you can generate the other digits. Suppose the spectator gives you the digit 5. You find out that it's the third digit. The fourth digit, then, must be one more than this. So the fourth digit is 6. Subtract 6 from 10, and you get the first digit, 4. Subtract 1 from 4, and you get the second digit, 3. The entire number, then, is 4356.

Play the Odds

Like many excellent tricks, this one is deceptively simple. The perfect foil, then, is Jim, who is deceptively bright.

All you need are five slips of paper (the sizes need not be uniform) and a writing instrument. On the first slip, jot down 1 on one side, and 2 on the other. On the second slip, write 3 on one side, 4 on the other. The third slip has 5 on one side, 6 on the other. The fourth has 7 on one side, 8 on the other. The fifth has 9 on one side, 10 on the other.

As you mark them, say to Jim, "I wonder if you'd assist me in an experiment. We'll find out if even the slightest clue can somehow enable me to see with my mind what I cannot see with my eyes."

Hand the slips to Jim.

"These slips have numbers on both sides. In fact, the numbers run from 1 to 10. In a moment, I'll turn my back. When I do, I'd like you to mix these slips any way you want to. You can shuffle them up, turn some over, whatever you want to do. Then I'd like you to just drop them on the table so that even you won't have any idea of what numbers are likely to be up. Tell me when you're done."

You turn away while Jim mixes the slips. When he's ready, you ask, "I think I can tell you the total showing on the slips, Jim. But I'm not absolutely sure. I'll need one clue. How many of the slips have an odd number showing?"

He tells you. You give this information considerable thought and finally tell him the total showing on all five slips. Actually, you could have told him the total immediately, but that wouldn't be good technique.

It's really quite simple. You subtract the number he gives you from 30. If he tells you that three of the slips have an odd number, for instance, you subtract 3 from 30, getting 27. The total of all five slips will be 27.

How about a repeat? Doing the trick again can actually throw the spectators off. The second time, after Jim mixes the slips, ask for the number of slips showing an even number. This really doesn't change anything. You merely use the even number to discover the number of slips with odd numbers showing. You do this by subtracting the even number from 5. You subtract the result from 30.

For example, Jim tells you that one of the slips shows an even number. Clearly, four slips must show an odd number (5-1=4). So just subtract 4 from 30 to get the correct total.

Performing the trick twice is just about right. If you decide to do it a third time, it will be more deceptive if you again ask for the number of even slips showing.

Why It Works: Take a look at the five slips with all five showing odd numbers:

$$\underline{1} \quad \underline{3} \quad \underline{5} \quad \underline{7} \quad \underline{9}$$
$$2 \quad 4 \quad 6 \quad 8 \quad 10$$

The total of the odd numbers is 25 (1+3+5+7+9=25). Assume that you turn over any one of the slips. What happens? The total increases by one. So when there are four odd numbers showing, the total will be 26. And it doesn't matter which one is turned over.

Suppose you turn the slip over which has 7 on one side and 8 on the other. Four odd numbers are showing, and the total is increased by one. (30-4=26). Let's turn over an additional slip—let's say the one with 3 on one side and 4 on the other. Now, three odd numbers are showing, and the total is 27 (30-3=27).

If you turn over two more slips (for a total of four), only one odd number will show, and the total will increase by two more (30-1=29).

And if you turn over all the slips, no odd number will be showing, and the total will be 30 (30-0=30).

PREDICTION

Magician's Choice

The "magician's choice" is a subtle device in which a spectator apparently has free choice, but actually is forced to take *your* choice. Let's try it out in a quick prediction trick.

"I'm going to attempt to tell the future." Greg is a staunch believer in astrology, so he's delighted to assist you. "First, my prediction." Making sure that no one can see what you write, jot down the number 5 on a piece of paper. Fold the paper and set it aside.

On another sheet of paper, print the digits 1 to 9 in a row. Hand Greg the pencil and paper. "Greg, I'd like you to cross out one of the digits." Odds are pretty good that he'll cross out 5. If he does, have him open the prediction and announce the digit you've jotted there.

Suppose he crosses out a different digit. Mutter, "It'll take too long if we do them one at a time." Aloud, say, "Let's speed things up. Name four other digits, Greg."

If, among the digits, he names 5, say, "Fine. Good choices. Now, cross out the rest of the digits." This leaves you with four digits, one of which is 5.

If, however, he does not name 5 as one of the digits, say, "Good. Cross out those digits, please." Again, you're left with four digits, one of which is 5.

You should phrase the next elimination exactly like this: "This time I'd like you to choose two of the remaining digits. Name two of the digits."

Greg names two digits. If one of them is 5, say, "Good. Cross out the other two."

If neither is 5, say, "Good. Cross those out."

You're down to two digits. "We have two digits left—one for me, and one for you. Which one do you want for yourself?"

If he says 5, say, "Okay, that's yours. Cross out the other one."

If he names the other digit, say, "Okay. Cross that out. That leaves me with 5."

Without pausing, continue, "So we're down to one digit, 5. Please open my prediction and read it aloud."

Why It Works: The success of any "magician's choice" trick depends upon how natural the elimination seems to the onlookers. With this one, it's vital that you act promptly each time you eliminate a digit. This means that you must know exactly how to react when each choice is made. Although the trick itself is quite simple, you must practice until the various alternatives become second nature to you.

Tallying the Future

"Once more, I'm going to try to look into the future." Without letting anyone else see what you're writing, jot down a two-digit number on a piece of paper. Let's say that you jot down 35. (The number must be from 10 to 39.) Fold the paper and have a spectator hold it for safekeeping.

Perhaps Janet will be kind enough to assist you. "Janet, I want you to arrive at a number by chance, not through some sort of psychological stunt. Let's start by having you jot down some number between 50 and 100. Don't let me see what you write."

Let's say that Janet jots down the number 82.

Your prediction, in this instance 35, is subtracted from 99. 99-35=64.

(If you haven't done the subtraction in advance, an easy way to do it is to subtract the prediction number from 100 and subtract 1 from the result.)

You'll want Janet to add this amount, 64, to her chosen number. Phrase it like this:

"Janet, I'd like you add something fairly substantial to your number— oh, say, 64. Yes, add 64 to your number."

Janet's number is 82. She adds 64 to this, getting 146.

"Cross off the first digit of your answer." She does, getting 46.

"That digit that you crossed off—add that to your number." She crossed off 1, so she adds 1 to her number, getting 47.

"Subtract that amount from your original number." 82-47=35.

"This is the random number you've chosen. Please check my prediction." She does. It matches her freely chosen number.

Another example: You jot down a prediction, using a number from 10 to 39. Let's say that the prediction is 26. You give Janet these instructions:

1) Write down any number from 50 to 100. (She writes down 59.)

2) Add 73 to your number. (73 is your prediction amount [26] subtracted from 99. She adds 59 and 73, getting 132.)

3) Cross off the first digit of your answer. (She crosses off the 1, leaving 32.)

4) Add that digit to your total. (She adds 1 to 32, getting 33.)

5) Subtract that amount from your original number. (She subtracts 33 from 59, getting 26—the number you predicted.)

Why It Works: In some ways, this is an example of "give-and-take,"which is explained at the end of "Birthday Change," pages 10-12, and "More Info," pages 12-14. The basic principle used here, however, is much more subtle. Let me use the last example to explain.

We'll work backwards. You want to end up with 26. How do you do this? Well, Janet has chosen a number—in this instance, 59. If you should subtract 33 from 59, you'll get 26. But how do you get 33?

The inventor of this trick had a brainstorm. He figured that you could do some extraordinarily slick things with the number 99. You could, for instance, divide it into two pieces—26 and 73. The first piece is the prediction; the second piece is added to the spectator's chosen number. You now have three significant numbers:

26-the prediction, a portion of 99.

73-added to spectator's number, the other portion of 99.

59-the spectator's chosen number.

Possibly, the inventor thought this: What if I subtract 99 from the total of the spectator's number and the number I gave her, 73? Here's what would happen:

$$59 + 73 = 132$$
$$132 - 99 = 33$$

33! We know exactly what to do with 33. We subtract it from Janet's number, 59, to get your prediction, 26.

So what's the clever thing that the inventor came up with? He worked out a way to subtract 99 without anyone being aware of what's going on. Always, the total of the spectator's number and the one you give her will end up with a three digit number beginning with 1.

So you say to Janet, "Cross off the first digit of your answer." You're acting as though this could be any digit. Also, when she crosses off the 1, she automatically subtracts 100 from her total. You continue, "That digit that you crossed off—add that to your number." She does so; the total effect is that she has subtracted 99.

Obviously, the inventor could have originally subtracted his prediction from 100 and then later have the spectator cross off the first number. But this method is much more clever, and gives the impression that the crossed-off number could be any digit.

Note: Why must your prediction be from 10 to 39, and the spectator's number be from 50 to 100? The answer is absurdly simple. The trick won't work with other numbers. (Make your prediction 40, for instance, and see what happens. Or, make the spectator's number 49 or 101 and see what happens.)

BOOK TESTS

Completely by Chance

One of the best book tests is this one, attributed to Richard Himber. You must have three books—paperbacks will be fine. And, of course, you'll need pencil and paper. One of the three books will be your key book. Turn to page 43 of this book and memorize the first line.

Start by setting the three books in a row on a table. The key book should be in the middle (Illus. 16). Say, "Let's try an experiment with these books. I'll need a volunteer."

Illus. 16

Leona is an avid reader, so she should be happy to be participating in this test.

"Leona, please pick up one of the books—any one—it doesn't matter." If you're casual enough, Leona will probably pick the middle one, the key book. Suppose, however, she picks up a different book. "All right, you've picked a book. Now I'll pick one."

Two books are on the table. Pick up the one which is not the key book. "Now we each have a book to work with."

Turn to Patrick. "Would you please take the remaining book and go into the next room with it." Or you could ask Patrick to take the book across the room.

You want to force the number 43, of course. You start by mentally subtracting 43 from 100, getting 57. You'll now use that number. Open the cover of your book. From the beginning, start slowly riffling through the pages. "Leona, please tell me when to stop."

She does. Look at the right-hand page and announce, "57. Would you please jot that down, Leona." Obviously, you should try to time it so that you stop riffling at a point where the page could actually be number 57.

Leona jots down 57.

"That's my number, Leona. You should also pick a number, so that we end up with a number chosen completely at random. I'll turn away. You riffle through your book and stop wherever you wish. But make sure you stop somewhere beyond my number. We might as well end up with a good-sized number. On the other hand, it shouldn't be too big, so make sure your number is less than 100, okay?"

Turn away while Leona does this. "Do you have a number? Good. Please write it down below my number. And then add the two numbers together."

Suppose that Leona has settled on page number 83. She adds 83 to your 57: $57+83=140$.

"Is your answer a three-digit number?" Yes. "I was afraid of that. We may have too big a number. Why don't you just cross off the first digit." While she does this, you mutter, "Let's see, what else can we do? I've got it!" Say aloud, "Leona, you now have a two-digit number. Subtract that from the number that you chose. Now, that's your page number. What could be fairer?" Practically anything.

Leona subtracts 40 from 83 and gets 43.

"Leona, please go into the other room and tell Patrick the page number you chose. Then both of you return."

When they come back, say, "Patrick, please open your book to the page number that Leona chose."

Your back should be to your two assistants.

"Don't forget now: The book was freely chosen, and the page number was freely chosen. I'd like both Patrick and Leona to look at the first line on that chosen page. Please concentrate on that line."

With considerable strain, you proceed to read the line. You don't read the line exactly, however. Instead, you reverse the position of some words, and you get one or two words wrong—similar but not quite right. This, of course, is to be expected when you attempt a feat of mind reading. After you stagger through your rendition, repeat it. Then ask one of your assistants to read the actual first line. It turns out that you're astonishingly close.

Why It Works: Let's illustrate with the numbers used above. You arbitrarily decided to use page 43. Your job, then, is to force 43 on Leona.

First, subtract 43 from 100, getting 57.Pretend to flip to page 57 and ask Leona to jot down the number. Then turn away and ask Leona to flip through her book and find a number between 57 and 100. She chooses 83.

Leona adds these two numbers together: 57+83=140.

At this point, you know that the answer is a three-digit number beginning with the digit 1. Pretending that you may have too big a number, you have Leona cross off the first digit. In other words, she subtracts 100 from her answer. What she now has is 40.

What does this 40 represent? When you had her subtract 100, she automatically got rid of your 57. And, because 57 subtracted from 100 is 43, she also dropped 43 from the final number. So this final number is actually Leona's original number minus 43. Therefore, when she subtracts this from her original number, she gets 43.

Odds or Evens

Martin Gardner invented this simple but baffling trick. I have added a slight variation.

This is an entirely different sort of book test from the previous one. You will need any book and two volunteers. Gladys and Tom are willing, so hand one of them the book. Let's say that Gladys has the book.

Turn away and say, "Gladys, I'd like you and Tom to assist me in an easy experiment. Please open the book to any page and set it onto the table. Now you have two pages to look at—one on the left and one on the right. Gladys, please put your hand on either the left page or the right page. And Tom, please put your hand on the other page."

Pause. "To make things more confusing, Gladys, I'd like you to look at the number of your page and multiply that by 5. Tom, I want you to multiply your page number by 10. Now, one of you add those two results together."

They may need paper and a writing instrument, so make sure these are available. Wait a moment. "Please make sure your hand is on the proper page so that I can get a mental picture of it. So what number did you end up with?"

Suppose the answer is 365.

You announce, "Gladys, I see a picture of your hand on the right page. And, naturally, Tom has his hand on the left page."

How do you know? When the answer ends in an odd number, as above, the spectator who multiplied by an odd number will have her hand on the odd page. (When you look at an open book, the page with the odd number is always on the right, of course.) When the answer ends in an even number, the spectator who multiplied by an odd number will have her hand on the even page. (The even-numbered page is always the page on the left.)

Odd multiplier, odd answer=odd page.

Odd multiplier, even answer=even page.

You need not have the spectators multiply by 10 and 5. It is only important that one of the numbers be even and the other odd. And you must know which participant is multiplying by the odd number. In the above example, Gladys multiplied by the odd number. This made her the key participant. If the answer was odd, her page was odd; if the answer was even, her page was even.

After doing the trick once, say, "Of course, I had a 50-percent chance of being right. Let's try again. Open the book to another page, please. And each of you choose a side on which to place your hand."

You may simply repeat the trick exactly as described above. I like to throw a little magic dust in their eyes by complicating things. Remember, the only essential is that one must multiply by an odd number, and the other by an even number. So I might say, "Gladys, this time multiply the number of your page by 7, a very lucky number. And Tom, what number would you choose to multiply by?" If he chooses an even number, fine; tell him to go ahead. If he chooses an odd number, say, "No that's too easy. Double that, and then multiply."

The trick should be done at least three times, so the next time you might let them both choose their numbers to multiply by. First, Gladys chooses. Let's say she chooses an odd number. If luck is with you, Tom chooses an even number, and you're all set. But if he chooses an odd number also, you simply have him double it, as above.

Suppose Gladys chooses an even number. Again, you hope Tom will take an odd number, but if he doesn't, say, "Let's throw a little luck into the picture. Add 7 to your number, Tom, and then multiply."

Once more, the secret: A book is laid open. Each of two spectators touches a different page. You have one spectator multiply the page number by an even number and the other multiply the page number by an odd number. The spectators add their results together and give you the result.

Remember which spectator multiplied by the odd number. This is the key participant. If the result ends in an odd number, the key participant is touching the odd page—the page on the right. If the result ends in an even number, that spectator is touching the even page—the one on the left.

Why It Works: Any number, odd or even, when multiplied by an even number will produce an even number. To get an odd number, you must multiply two odd numbers.

You tell Spectator 1 to multiply her page number by 5 (or any other odd number). If the result is odd, she must have her hand on an odd-numbered page—the page on the right. If the result is even, then she must have multiplied her odd number by an even number, so her hand is on an even-numbered page—the page on the left.

How about Spectator 2's multiplication with the even number? Irrelevant. The result will always be an even number. So when this number is added to Spectator 1's result, nothing changes. An even number added to an even number will produce another even number; an even number added to an odd number will produce an odd number.

FUN STUFF

It All Adds Down

Write this column of figures and ask someone to add them up one line at a time:

$$
\begin{array}{r}
1000 \\
20 \\
1030 \\
1000 \\
1030 \\
20 \\
\end{array}
$$

Before we go any further, why don't you give it a try.

Done? Good. What answer did you get? 5000? Good! You just proved that even extraordinarily bright people will get this wrong.

The correct answer is 4100. Don't feel bad; the vast majority get it wrong.

For best effect, jot down the column of numbers on the back of a calling card. When you show the stunt to someone, use another calling card to reveal the top number first, then the second number, and so on (Illus. 17).

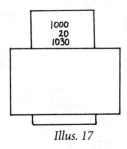

Illus. 17

Why It Works: As if you didn't know! You went like this:

1000	"One thousand...
20	...one thousand twenty...
1030	...two thousand fifty...
1000	...three thousand fifty...
1030	...four thousand eighty...
20	...five thousand."

After progressing through one, two, three, and four thousand, the tendency to go to five thousand is almost irresistible. Of course you know that 80+20=100, but the misdirection is just too strong.

Please State Your City

As long as you're marking up calling cards, you might want to jot this number down on one (Illus. 18): 51041771.

Illus. 18

Show the number to a friend and ask, "Why would this be the perfect number for someone from Chicago?" "No idea," he responds.

Have your chum turn the card upside down.

Of course, you could use a calculator instead of a card.

Still Hungry?

Dig around in your wallet. Surely you have yet another calling card. Jot down the number shown in Illus. 19.

Illus. 19

To perform the stunt, explain, "On his way out of a restaurant, a man stopped by the cashier. He handed her his napkin. This is what he had written on it."

Show the calling card to the onlookers. "What do you think it says?"

Someone who's quite bright will probably get the right answer. It doesn't matter, for you'll eventually provide the solution anyway: "I owe nothing, for I ate nothing."

All Together Now

This trick can be wonderful fun for a group. The basic idea is quite old, but Ed Hesse added some deceptive touches.

In preparation, you must write down on a card the number which is double the present year. For instance, a person who had performed the trick in 1996 would have written down 3,992 (1996×2). (It's a small point, but make sure you include the comma after the first digit so that people will be less likely to suspect the actual derivation of the number.)

In performance, make sure everyone in the group has a writing instrument and paper. Then provide these instructions:

1) Please write down the year you were born.

2) Below this, jot down the year of a memorable event—your marriage, your graduation, your discharge from service, whatever.

3) Below this, write down the age you are or will be on your birthday this year.

4) Finally, write down the number of years since that memorable event at the end of this year.

5) Add up all your numbers.

When everyone is done, hold up the card on which you've written your number so that everyone can see it. "How many of you have this number?"

Just about everyone will have it. Only those who are poor at math will miss.

Why It Works: If you take the date on which an event occurred and add to it the number of years ago on which it occurred, you'll end up with this year's date. If you do this twice, you'll end up with a number which is twice this year's date. Which is exactly what happens here.

A Nickel for Your Thoughts

Hand Gary a penny and a nickel. "Gary, I'm going to turn my back. When I do, I'd like you to hold the penny in one hand and the nickel in the other hand."

Turn away. "Gary, please multiply the value of the coin in your left hand by 14." Pause a moment. "Ready?" If he tells you no, wait until he indicates he's ready to continue. If he says yes, proceed immediately.

"Now, multiply the value of the coin in your right hand by 14." He'll tell you when he's done.

"Please add the two numbers together and tell me the total." Unless Gary is seriously deficient in his addition skills, you'll always hear the total 84. You promptly tell him which hand holds what coin.

Since the total is always the same, how do you know this?

The answer is easy. Multiplying 14 by 1 is much easier than multiplying 14 by 5. You have Gary multiply the value of the coin in his left hand by 14. Pause briefly, and then say, "Ready?" If the answer is no, he holds the nickel in that hand. If the answer is yes, the penny is in his left hand.

The Sneaky Serpent

This clever trick is the invention of Karl Fulves.

Three objects are placed in a row on a table. A spectator mixes them. The magician gives the exact position of each object. A beautiful trick, with just one flaw: It works only 5 out of 6 times.

I have adapted the trick to playing cards and have added a devilish patter theme. This version works 6 out of 6 times.

If you wish, you may perform the trick over the phone. But let's suppose you're performing it for a group. Gilbert is a good sport, so ask him to help out.

"Gilbert, I'm going to turn my back in a moment." Hand him the deck of cards. "After I do, I'll provide you with some instructions. If all goes well, I may be able to perform a feat of mind reading."

Turn your back and provide these instructions, pausing at appropriate spots:

"Please take from the deck the K and Q of any suit. These will stand for Adam and Eve. They are, of course, in the Garden of Eden. What's missing? Why, the snake! So please take out the AS (Ace of Spades), who will be Satan, the sneaky serpent. Set the rest of the deck aside.

"Please mix the three cards. Now turn them faceup and deal them into a row. You don't have them in A K Q order, do you?" If the answer is no, say, "I knew that." Then continue your instructions. If the answer is yes, say, "Please don't use that order—it's just too easy." Actually, when the cards are in A K Q order, the trick won't work.

Continue: "Start by switching the serpent with whoever is on his right. If the serpent is on the right end, just leave him be.

"Next, switch Eve with whoever is on her left. If she is at the left end, just leave her be.

"Finally, switch Adam for whoever is on his right. If he's on the right end, just leave him be."

When Gilbert finishes, say, "Let's see if we can arrange to keep Adam and Eve in the Garden of Eden. We'll have to get rid of the serpent. I wonder where he is. I know! It's obvious, isn't it? The serpent most certainly wants to come between Adam and Eve, so he must be in the middle. Please remove him from the middle so he'll stop bothering the happy couple. So there they are, side by side, just as though they're standing at the altar about to get married—Eve on the left, and Adam on the right."

Review:

1) Gilbert removes from the deck the K and Q of any suit, along with the AS.

2) He deals them in a row in any order. But you eliminate the A K Q order.

3) Gilbert makes three switches in this order:

The A for the card to its right.

The Q for the card to its left.

The K for the card to its right.

4) The three cards are now in this order: Q A K.

Why It Works: When you begin, there are 6 possible positions:

1) A K Q
2) A Q K
3) Q A K
4) Q K A
5) K A Q
6) K Q A

You verbally eliminate 1) because you know that, with this setup, the series of moves will not bring about the desired result.

You provide the first instruction: Exchange the A with the card on its right. After Gilbert does so, here are the only possible setups:

1) Q A K
2) Q K A
3) K Q A

The second instruction: Exchange the Q with the card on her left. Now there are only two possibilities:

1) Q A K
2) Q K A

The final instruction: Exchange the K with card on his right. Only one possibility remains:

Q A K

As you can see, in just three clever moves, you've eliminated all possibilities except the desired one.

Notes:

1) The trick may be enhanced if you hesitate and stammer a bit as you provide the directions, creating the impression that you're simply making up each move as you go along. "Let's see. Let's try Eve—the queen. How about exchanging her—oh, I don't know...Maybe...yeah...How about exchanging her for the card on her left."

2) To make sure the trick works, you more or less tell Gilbert not to use the A K Q order. There's at least one other way you can eliminate the A K Q order.

Before providing instructions for the three switches, say, "When you put your three cards in a row, make sure that the serpent is to the right of Adam or Eve—either one. You see, Satan likes to tempt by whispering in the left ear." Then proceed with the instructions, as above.

LIGHTNING CALCULATION

The Speedy Adder

Does the name Leonardo Fibonacci strike a responsive chord in you? Possibly not. It is time for a brief history lesson. This late 12th- and early-13th-century Italian mathematician made amazing discoveries in his field. He is best known, however, for a number sequence known as the Fibonacci series, in which each number is the total of the two previous numbers.

For instance, a number is written down. Another number is written beneath it. The two are added together, and the total placed beneath the second number. Then the second number and the third number are added together and this total is put down below the third number. The sequence can go on indefinitely.

Of what use is this? Using this series, you can perform an astonishing lightning calculation—or at least appear to do so.

If you like, you can introduce the stunt by briefly discussing Fibonacci. Or you might just explain how to develop a Fibonacci series without naming it. Usually, I prefer the latter.

"We're going to develop a rather large number totally by chance. I'll show you how."

Ask someone to name a small number. Jot it down. Suppose the number is 8.

8

Ask someone else to name a different small number. Let's say the number is 13.

8
13

"Eight and 13 is 21," you point out. "So that would become the next number." You now have this:

8
13
21

"How do we get the next number? We just add the last two together. In this instance, we have 13 and 21. We add them together, and we get 34."

You now have this on your paper:

$$8$$
$$13$$
$$21$$
$$34$$

To make sure someone understands, it's time for a brief quiz. "So what would the next number be?" Sure enough, several have worked out that you add 21 and 34 together, getting 55.

Now you're ready to get down to business. Toss your worksheet away. On another sheet, put a column of numbers from 1 to 10 with a dash after each figure (Illus. 20). This has a dual purpose. It makes sure that your assistants put down exactly 10 numbers, and—as you'll see—because you need to be able to spot the 7th number at a glance.

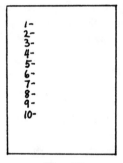

Illus. 20

Ask Rudy and Julie to assist you. "In a moment, I'll turn my back. After I do, I'd like you each to think of a number. Rudy, think of a number from 5 to 15. Julie, you think of one from 10 to 20. Rudy, please put your number after number 1 on the sheet. Julie, you put yours after number 2 on the sheet. Then we'll have Julie do the hard work. She'll add the two numbers and put the total after number 3 on the sheet. Then she'll continue, all the way down to 10. Rudy, you can be the official referee. Make sure Julie doesn't accidentally put down a wrong number. After you're done, I'll try to add up the column of numbers as quickly as I can."

Turn away while the two do their math exercise. When they're done, turn back. Take the writing instrument and draw a line under the column of figures. After a quick glance down the column, jot down the total. Just as with regular addition, you put in the digits, moving from right to left.

Ask Rudy to add the column and put his answer below yours. Sure enough, his answer is identical to yours.

How do you do it? Nothing to it. Just multiply the 7th number by 11. Please! No crying about, "I'm no good at multiplying in my head." Of course you're not. Neither am I. That's why I worked out an easy way for me to multiply by 11 without hurting my head bone. Let's take a look at a typical Fibonacci series (Illus. 21).

Illus. 21

The correct total is 1386. You can arrive at this total quickly by multiplying the 7th number (126) by 11. First, understand that, with the limitations placed on the choice of numbers, you'll always end up with a four-digit number. Furthermore, the 7th number will always be a three-digit number.

So you're working with the 7th number, 126. If you were to simply multiply by 11, it would look like this:

$$\begin{array}{r} 126 \\ \times 11 \\ \hline 126 \\ 126 \\ \hline 1386 \end{array}$$

As you can see, the first digit on the right will always be the same in both numbers. In this instance, the digit is 6. So you put this down on the right, below the column of figures.

6

To get the digit to the left of this, you add the second and third digits together. The number is 126; we add the 6 and 2, getting 8. So we put down 8 to the left of the 6.

86

How do we get the first two digits? Consider the first two digits of the 7th number. The 7th number is 126, and the first two digits form the number 12. We add to this the first digit, 1. 12+1=13.

1 3 8 6

Let's try another example (Illus. 22).

The correct answer is 2497. The 7th number is 227. So the number on the far right will be 7.

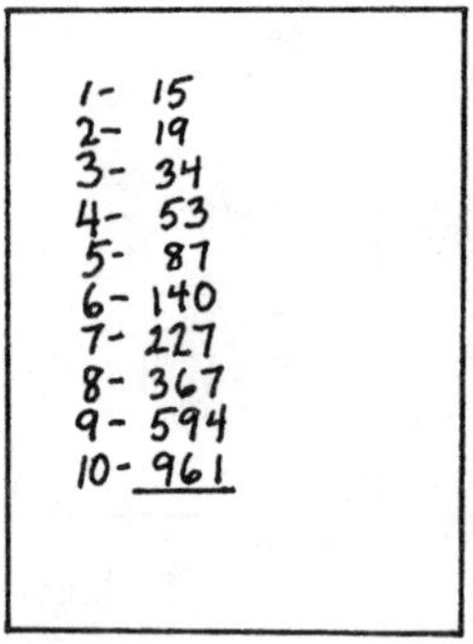

1- 15
2- 19
3- 34
4- 53
5- 87
6- 140
7- 227
8- 367
9- 594
10- 961

Illus. 22

Add the last two digits of 227. 2+7=9. So 9 is the next digit to the left: 97.

Take the first two digits of 227, and you get the number 22. Add the first digit, which is 2, and you get 24: 2497.

Let's try one more example to illustrate an exception (Illus. 23).

The correct answer is 1848. The 7th number is 168, so the digit on the far right will be an 8.

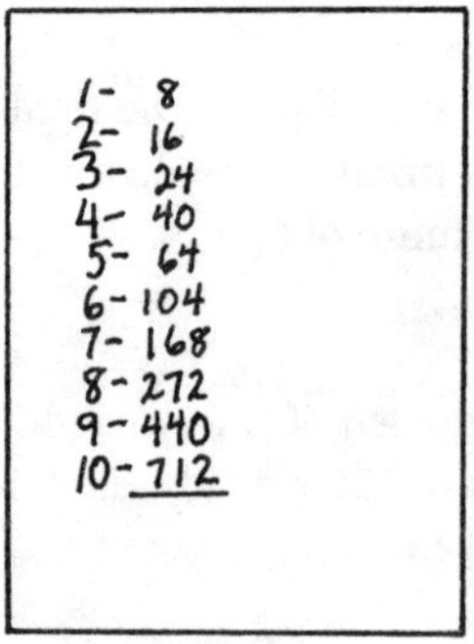

1- 8
2- 16
3- 24
4- 40
5- 64
6- 104
7- 168
8- 272
9- 440
10- 712

Illus. 23

The last two digits of 168 are 6 and 8. We add them and get 14. In the previous examples, we had one digit; here we have a two-digit number. No problem, however. You treat it exactly like any other addition; that is, you enter the 4, and you carry the 1: 48

The first two digits of 168 form the number 16. To this, you add the 1 that you're carrying. 16+1=17. Now, you add to this the first digit, which is also a 1. 17+1=18: 1848.

Summary:

Two spectators construct a Fibonacci series of 10 numbers. You pretend to add the numbers, but actually multiply the 7th number in the series by 11. This is easy, because you don't have to remember any numbers; you simply look at the 7th number and work out the answer bit by bit.

1) The 7th number will contain three digits.

2) Put down the last digit as the last digit of your answer. If the 7th number is 125, you put down 5 as the digit on the far right.

3) As with regular addition, you place the next digit to the left of the first digit. You get this digit by adding together the 2nd and 3rd digits of the 7th number. Still assuming that the 7th number is 125, we add together the 2 and 5, getting 7. Put 7 to the left of the 5: 75.

4) The first two digits of 125 form the number 12. Add to this the first digit, in this instance 1. 12+1=13. So put down 13 to the left of the other two digits: 1375.

The only exception:

1) Assume that the 7th number is 194. Put down the 4 on the right.

2) Add the last two digits, getting 13. Put down the 3 and carry the 1: 34.

3) The first two digits form the number 19. Add in the number you carried. 19+1=20. Now, as before, add the first digit to your total. 20+1=21. Put this down to the left: 2134.

Why It Works: Obviously, each number in a Fibonacci series is a fraction of the total. It happens that the 7th number is always precisely 1/11th of the final total. No other number in the series provides a consistent result.

Who figured this out, and how? Ahhh...I have a better idea. Take a card, look at it, remember it, put it back.

That's right. I don't know!

An Additional Trick

This is an excellent follow-up to the previous trick. The effect is similar, but the method is completely different. I have changed the original trick a trifle to make it more deceptive.

Say to Roger, "Let's take turns putting down numbers. Then we'll see how fast I can add them up. Let's start by putting down a 5-digit number."

He does so. You write a number below it. But your number is quite special (Illus. 24).

54296
45704

Illus. 24

As you put down your number from left to right, you make sure that each digit adds to 9 with the digits just above it. For instance, Roger's first digit is 5. You subtract 5 from 9, getting 4. So your first digit is 4.

You do something different for the last digit on the right. You make sure that your digit adds to 10 with the digit above it. Roger has a 6 as his last digit. You subtract this from 10, getting 4. So you put down 4 as your last digit.

Have Roger jot down another 5-digit number below the first two. He does so, and the sheet might look like that in Illus. 25.

54296
45704
93478

Illus. 25

You place a number below this, again making sure that each of the first four digits totals 9 with the digit above it, and that the last digit totals 10 with the digit above it (Illus. 26).

Since Roger's first number is a 9, you put nothing below the digit. Just casually say, "I think I'll try a four-digit number." If one of Roger's interior numbers were a 9, you would place a zero below it.

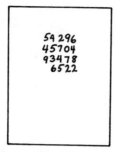

54 296
45704
93478
6522

Illus. 26

Again Roger jots down a 5-digit number, and you place a number below it (Illus. 27).

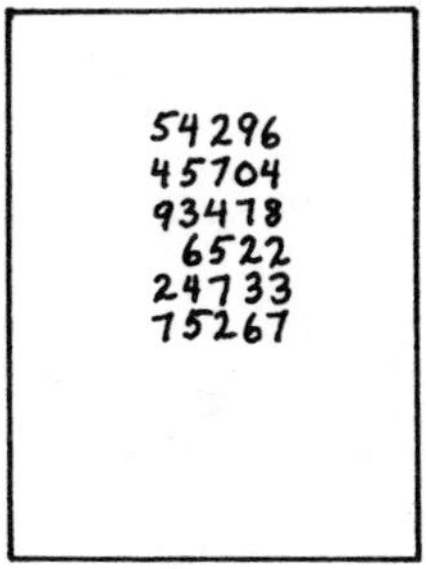

54296
45704
93478
6522
24733
75267

Illus. 27

Finally, you say to Roger, "Why don't you put down the last two numbers yourself. To make it harder, put a 5-digit number on top of the column and put another 5-digit number at the bottom of the column. I'll turn away."

When Roger's done, turn back, and draw a line below the eight numbers. Then, just about as fast as you can write, jot down the correct total.

However did you manage that? You simply totaled the top and bottom numbers. When you were done, you placed a 3 at the left of your total.

Let's take a look at what Roger left you (Illus. 28).

The top number, which he just added, is 32457. The bottom number, which he also just added, is 56421. You add these two together, putting down your answer as you go.

$$\begin{array}{r} 32457 \\ +56421 \\ \hline 88878 \end{array}$$

You have placed one digit in each column, but you'll require 6 digits.

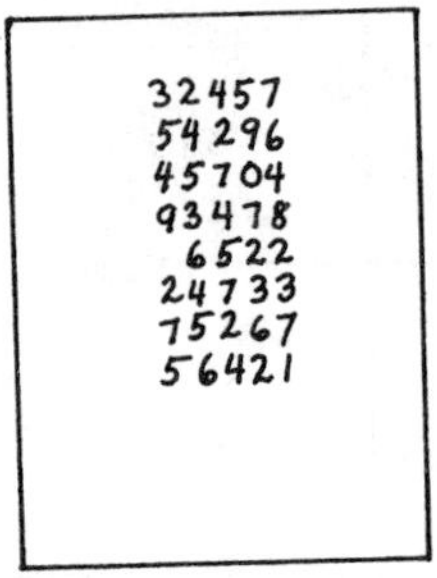

Illus. 28

So you place a 3 at the front of your total: 388878.

When Roger adds the columns to check your result, he finds that you're exactly right.

You'll always place a 3 at the front of your total, with one exception: Sometimes when you add together the last two digits, those at the extreme left, the result will be a two-digit number. For instance, the result might be 15. When this happens, you enter the second digit in the normal fashion. In this example, you'd jot down the 5. Then you add 3 to the first digit. Since the first digit is always 1, it means that the digit that you place at the front will be 4. Thus:

$$73481 — \text{Top number}$$
$$+95132 — \text{Bottom number}$$
$$468613$$

Let's try another example. The spectator has jotted down three 5-digit numbers; you have added a number below each one (Illus. 29).

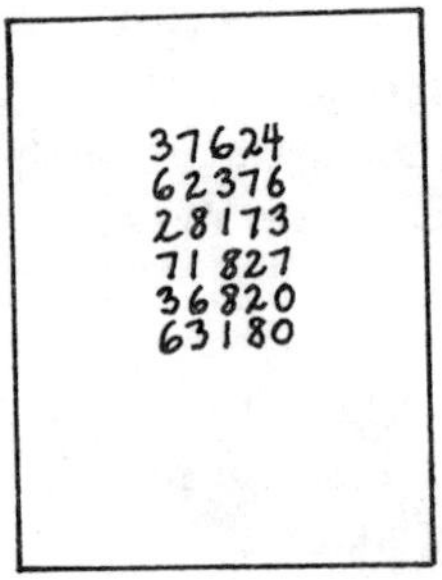

Illus. 29

Note the last two numbers in the column. The spectator wrote 36820. Immediately you notice that the spectator has placed a zero at the end of his number. You're supposed to place a digit there which will add to 10 with the digit above it. Obviously, the only digit that will do is another zero. But when you do this, you have to make sure that your next digit to the left will add to 10 with the digit above it. So you simply start at the left and proceed through the first three digits in the regular way. You make sure that each of your digits adds up to 9 with the digit above it. When you reach the fourth digit from the left(the 2, in this instance), you make sure that your digit adds up to 10 with the digit above it. Finally, put a zero at the end.

The spectator adds two more 5-digit numbers, one above the others and one below the others (Illus. 30).

Illus. 30

You draw a line under the column. Then you add together the number at the top of the column and the number at the bottom of the column. Going from right to left, you perform the first four additions:

$$81014$$
$$+98341$$
$$\overline{9355}$$

The two digits to be added at the far left are 8 and 9. Add them together, getting 17. When you have a two-digit number, enter the second digit—in this instance, 7. Then place a 4 in front of the entire number:

$$81014$$
$$+98341$$
$$\overline{479355}$$

Why It Works: The spectator writes down a 5-digit number; you write a number beneath it. You make sure that each of your first four digits adds to 9 with the digit above it, and that the last digit adds to 10 with the digit above it:

37862

62138

Because of what you have done, these two numbers add up to 100,000.

You go through the procedure twice more, each time guaranteeing that the total of the two numbers will add up to 100,000.

At this point, you have six numbers entered, and the total of these numbers is 300,000. You turn away, and your assistant puts down two more numbers.

When you turn back, here's what you actually do: You add together the last two numbers that the spectator put down, and you add to that 300,000.

Obviously, you add the 300,000 by placing a 3 in front of the total, or, if the last addition amounts to 10 or more, by placing a 4 in front of the total.

Note: When the spectator puts in his last two numbers, you have him place one on top of the column, and one on the bottom. Why not have him put both at the bottom? If they're both at the bottom, a spectator might more readily see that you're adding the two together.

MEMORY TRICKS

Serial Number Scam

Gary usually carries money with him. Ask him to hand you a bill of any denomination. "In just a few seconds, I'll memorize the serial numbers," you say.

You take the bill and look at the serial numbers. As usual when performing your little tricks, you have stretched the truth; you don't actually memorize the serial numbers. Instead, add them up and then reduce them to a single digit. For instance, you might have these numbers: 73824245. It's certainly no problem adding them up: 7+3+8+2+4+2+4+5=35. You still have two digits, so add these together: 3+5=8. Now you've reduced the serial number to 8. Remember this digit.

Return the bill to Gary and hand him a pen. "When I turn away, I'd like you to circle any one of the digits in the serial number."

After he does so, keep your back turned, and tell him, "Please read the rest of the digits in the serial number. In other words, read all the digits except the one you circled. Please read them slowly, because I have to really concentrate."

For a change, you are telling the precise truth; you really must concentrate. As he reads off the numbers, you add them together. Following our example, suppose Gary reads off these digits: 7824245.

You add them as he goes along: 7+8+2+4+2+4+5=32. You reduce the answer to a single digit: 3+2=5.

"All right," you say. "The digit you circled is 3."

Wow! What a memory! All you really remembered, however, was that first digit, 8. Then you subtracted the second digit from it. 8-3=5.

Let's try another example. Gary hands you another bill. You note that the serial number is 45864354. You add up the bill's digits: 4+5+8+6+4+3+5+4=39. You still have two digits, so you add these together: 3+9=12. Doggone it! you still have two digits. So you add the 1 and 2, getting 3. Now you've reduced the serial number to 3. Remember this digit.

While your back is turned, Gary circles one of the digits. Then he slowly tells you the other digits. You add them as he goes along: 4+5+8+6+4+3+4=34. You reduce the answer to a single digit: 3+4=7.

Next, you subtract the second digit from the first. But that won't work.

The first digit is 3, and the second digit is 7. So what do you do? Add 9 to the first digit, and then subtract. The first digit is 3; we add 9 and get 12. We subtract 7 from 12, and get 5, which turns out to be the circled digit.

Why It Works: The description pretty much explains it. To further illustrate, let me construct a 6-digit number: 593274. The digits add up to 30. Reduced to a single digit, you get 3.

Now, let's add another digit, 6. As you can see, the single-digit result will now be 9. Drop the 6, and you end up with 3. Drop the 3, and you end up with 6.

Here's what happens: Add up a series of numbers and reduce the total to a single digit. Eliminate one of the digits in the series. Add up the series again and reduce the total to a single digit. Subtract the second digit from the first; the total will equal the value of the digit you eliminated.

When the first digit is smaller than the second, you add 9 to the first digit and then subtract. Why? Let's suppose that the first digit is 4, and the second is 7. You add 9 to the 4, getting 13. Now you subtract 7, getting 6, which turns out to be the missing number.

Actually, you're still subtracting 7 from 4. Adding 9 is just a convenient way of converting 4 to a two-digit number—in this instance, 13 (1+3=4). You could use any two digits that add up to 4. For instance, you could use 22 or 31. If you use 22, you subtract 7, getting 15; add the 1 and 5 and you get 6, the missing number. How about 31? Subtract 7 and you get 24; add the 2 and 4 and again you get 6.

Ah, Yes, I Remember It Well

You present a chart on which you have typed anywhere from 20 to 40 lines of digits. My chart consists of 20 lines, double-spaced. Each line contains 20 digits. Here it is:

```
 (1)  4 5 9 4 3 7 0 7 7 4 1 5 6 1 7 8 5 3 8 1
 (2)  7 9 6 5 1 6 7 3 0 3 3 6 9 5 4 9 3 2 5 7
 (3)  6 9 5 4 9 3 2 5 7 2 9 1 0 1 1 2 3 5 8 3
 (4)  9 3 2 5 7 2 9 1 0 1 1 2 3 5 8 3 1 4 5 9
 (5)  8 3 1 4 5 9 4 3 7 0 7 7 4 1 5 6 1 7 8 5
 (6)  1 7 8 5 3 8 1 9 0 9 9 8 7 5 2 7 9 6 5 1
 (7)  0 7 7 4 1 5 6 1 7 8 5 3 8 1 9 0 9 9 8 7
 (8)  3 1 4 5 9 4 3 7 0 7 7 4 1 5 6 1 7 8 5 3
 (9)  2 1 3 4 7 1 8 9 7 6 3 9 2 1 3 4 7 1 8 9
(10)  5 6 1 7 8 5 3 8 1 9 0 9 9 8 7 5 2 7 9 6
(11)  4 6 0 6 6 2 8 0 8 8 6 4 0 4 4 8 2 0 2 2
```

```
(12) 7 0 7 7 4 1 5 6 1 7 8 5 3 8 1 9 0 9 9 8
(13) 6 0 6 6 2 8 0 8 8 6 4 0 4 4 8 2 0 2 2 4
(14) 9 4 3 7 0 7 7 4 1 5 6 1 7 8 5 3 8 1 9 0
(15) 8 4 2 6 8 4 2 6 8 4 2 6 8 4 2 6 8 4 2 6
(16) 1 8 9 7 6 3 9 2 1 3 4 7 1 8 9 7 6 3 9 2
(17) 0 8 8 6 4 0 4 4 8 2 0 2 2 4 6 0 6 6 2 8
(18) 3 2 5 7 2 9 1 0 1 1 2 3 5 8 3 1 4 5 9 4
(19) 2 2 4 6 0 6 6 2 8 0 8 8 6 4 0 4 4 8 2 0
(20) 5 7 2 9 1 0 1 1 2 3 5 8 3 1 4 5 9 4 3 7
```

Each digit on the chart is generated by totaling the two previous dig-its. For instance, on Line 16, you see that the first two digits are 1 and 8. Obviously, 1+8=9. So the next digit is 9: 189.

Now, you total 9 and 8, getting 17. But you use only the second digit, 7:1897.

If you look over the chart, you'll see that all the numbers are generat-ed this way.

Hand the chart to Larry, saying, "I've memorized all these lines, Larry. It took me months and months, but I think it was worth it to be able to demonstrate my superb memory."

You turn your back, saying, "Pick out a line, Larry, and tell me which one it is." He tells you. You immediately tell him all the digits on the line. The trick may be repeated.

How? The number of the line tips off all the remaining digits. First, let's assume that the number of the line is a single digit. If the number is odd, you add 3 to it; if the number is even, you add 5 to it. This gives you the first digit.

If Larry tells you he's looking at Line 5, you note that this is an odd number, so you add 3 to it. Your first digit, then, is 8.

You then add the number of the line to the first digit: 5+8=13. When you have a two-digit number, you always use the second digit only: 83.

Now, you're off and running. As explained earlier, once you know the first two digits, you can generate all the remaining digits.

Suppose that Larry's selected line is a single-digit *even* number. He chooses Line 4, for instance. You add 5, giving you 9.

You add 4 and 9, getting 13. Once more you use only the second digit, 3: 93.

Larry might choose a two-digit line. As with a single-digit line, you first add 3 to an odd number and 5 to an even number. For instance, Larry selects Line 13. You add 3 to this, getting 16. You use the 6 as the first digit.

To arrive at the next digit, however, you note the two digits in Larry's selection. In this instance, he chose line 13. You add the two digits together. This gives you 4. To this, you add the value of the first digit, 6. 6+4=10. You take the second digit; in this instance, you have a zero: 60.

Suppose Larry chooses an even two-digit number, like 16. You add 5 to it, getting 21. You use the second digit,1, as the first digit in the line.

Now, you add the digits in 16, getting 7. This, when added to the first digit, gives you 8: 18.

So, you have named the first two digits, and Larry is dumbfounded. You could go on naming digits forever, but that would give away the show. You'd better make sure you stop at 20. Since your back is to the spectators, keep track on your fingers. I start with my left thumb and move from left to right. After I hit my right thumb for the second time, I stop naming digits.

There's no reason you can't perform the trick again. But make sure you take the sheet back when you're finished. Given enough time, some clever rascal might figure out the code.

Notes:

1) Yes, yes, I can hear some of you whining, "Isn't there an easier way to get those first two digits?" Yes, there is. Larry tells you what line he chose. You concentrate and finally admit defeat: "I just can't seem to think of that first digit. What is it?" He tells you. You can now generate the second digit, as described above. Or, if you really don't want to strain yourself, admit to Larry that you can't get the second digit either. Now, you should be able to finish the line.

2) Practice doing several lines aloud. You'll find that it's surprisingly easy. The fact that you have just said two digits aloud keeps them fresh in your mind as you add them together to form the next digit.

As I Recall

I wish I knew who to credit for this clever pseudo-memory trick. Regardless, I've added a few refinements.

You'll need the assistance of Mary Lee, who is an excellent card shuffler. Hand her the deck, saying, "Please give these a good shuffle, Mary Lee, because I'd like to demonstrate my ability to memorize numbers."

When she finishes, take the deck back and set it facedown on the table. Hand Mary Lee a pencil and paper. "I'm not good at face cards [a king, queen, or jack], so we'll eliminate those. And I'm still working on suits [spades, hearts, diamonds, and clubs], so we'd better just confine ourselves to the values. Please jot these down in order."

Pick up the deck. Look at the top card, without letting anyone else see it. Give Mary Lee a number to write down; then place the card on the bottom of the deck. Continue doing this until you've provided some 20 numbers.

"Let's see if I can recall those numbers." Give the deck a quick shuffle, mumbling, "We'll make sure there's no chance I'll use the deck."

You then proceed to recite the numbers perfectly.

How can you possibly remember those numbers? You don't. You remember things like your social security number, an old phone number, a birth date.

Let's say your social security number is this: 372-06-9871. Obviously, you'll be able to remember this perfectly. So you simply recite this as you look at each card.

You look at the first card and say, "Three." You place the card on the bottom. You look at the next card and say, "Seven," and place that card on the bottom. You continue through the rest of your social security number. When you come to the zero, you convert it to 10. When you come to the 1, you convert it to ace.

So here are the first nine values you call out to Mary Lee: 3, 7, 2. 10, 6, 9, 8, 7, ace.

Let's say that a familiar phone number is 280-7156. You continue by calling out these values: 2, 8, 10, 7, ace, 5, 6.

Suppose there's a birth date which you know quite well—9/24/79, for instance. You recite these values: 9, 2, 4, 7, 9.

There you have 21 values which apparently you memorized just by glancing through the cards. What a genius! What a mind! What a hoax!

But don't get overconfident. You got away with it—good. But it's not advisable to repeat the trick. People might start to wonder why you're not showing them the cards.

Notes:

1) You've told the group that you'll skip face cards. As you come across a face card, toss it out faceup with a comment like, "No, face cards are too hard."

2) Quite often you'll name a number and, by coincidence, the card you're holding happens to be of that value. Let's say that you turn up the 2H just as you're about to announce the first digit of your phone number, which is also a 2. "Jot down two, please, Mary Lee." Show everyone the 2H, saying, "I won't forget the two of hearts; that's one of my lucky cards." Turn the card facedown and place it on the bottom.

If you're lucky enough to have this occur once or twice while calling out the numbers, the effect is considerably enhanced.

3) As I mentioned, you should use easily recalled numbers, like your social security number, a phone number, a birth date. You can also use a year, an address, or—if you were in service—your service number.

MAGIC SQUARES

An Easy Square

A typical magic square looks like the one shown in Illus. 31.

Notice that each column and each row adds up to 15. Also, each diagonal adds up to 15. First, let me explain how to construct this magic square. It may sound a bit complicated, but I'll show you an extremely easy way to construct it. Then I'll provide you with a spectacular trick which demonstrates your astonishing ability with numbers.

Start by putting the number 1 in the top middle space (Illus. 32). Then count 7 boxes to your next number. You count moving from left to right and then to the next lower box on the left...just as though you were reading. When you hit the seventh box, put in the next number, 2 (Illus. 33).

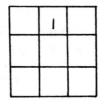

Illus. 31

Illus. 32

Illus. 33

Starting at the next box, the one at the top left, we count 4 to get to the next box, where we put in the next number, which is 3 (Illus. 34).

	1	
3		
		2

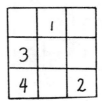

Illus. 34

Now, from the next box, we count 3 boxes for the placement of the next number, 4 (Illus. 35).

	1	
3		
4		2

Illus. 35

Then it's back to 7 boxes for the next number, 5 (Illus. 36).
Count 7 boxes again and put in the next number, 6 (Illus. 37).

	1	
3	5	
4		2

Illus. 36

	1	6
3	5	
4		2

Illus. 37

Count 3 boxes, putting in the next number, 7 (Illus. 38).
Count 4 boxes and put in the next number, 8 (Illus. 39).

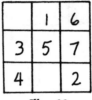

Illus. 38

	1	6
3	5	7
4		2

Illus. 39

8	1	6
3	5	7
4		2

Last of all, you would simply fill in the one empty box with the final number, 9. Actually, it is the 7th box from the preceding number.

To summarize the positioning of the numbers: The first number is placed in the middle box of the top line. After that, we count to succeeding numbers in this order: 7, 4, 3, 7, 7, 3, 4, 7.

The last four counts are a mirror image of the first four counts; this makes memorizing the numbers very easy. It also helps to note that the first number, 7, is followed by 4 and 3—two numbers which add up to 7.

Now you can construct a magic square containing the digits from 1 to 9. You can also now construct a magic square beginning with any number.

How would you present this as a trick? Depending on the size of the group, you can use either a large portable blackboard or a sheet of paper. Let's assume you're using paper and pen. Draw a square with nine empty boxes.

"Although you can't quite see it yet," you say, "this is a magic square. A magic square is one in which the numbers add up to the same total in every possible direction." At this point, have the group choose a representative. Address the nominee: "I'd like you to provide me with any number from 1 to 100. That will be the number I'll start the magic square with."

The spectator names a number, and you place it in the middle box on the top line. You put in succeeding numbers by counting to the appropriate boxes, as indicated. Suppose the number you're given is 82. It is placed as shown in Illus. 40.

The next number is placed 7 boxes away (Illus. 41).

You end up with the magic square shown in Illus. 42.

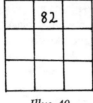

Illus. 40

Illus. 41

89	82	87
84	86	88
85	90	83

Illus. 42

You then show that, in every direction, the numbers add up to 258.

Notes:

1) You can have the spectators choose any number. The only reason you make it 1 to 100 is to speed up the trick. I have done 1 to 500, but have never quite dared to exhaust an audience's patience by making it 1 to 1000.

2) You're placing the numbers in the boxes right in front of the spectators, but try not to make it obvious that you're counting boxes to arrive at a succeeding number.

On the Square

Stephen Tucker invented a clever and entertaining trick, which makes up the first part of this demonstration. The latter part is a variation of one of Martin Gardner's creations.

On a sheet of paper or a blackboard, you've written this: $(? \times 4) + 34 =$

"Here we have a problem in algebra. Unfortunately, however, we have two unknowns, which would make this extremely difficult to solve."

Hand the sheet, along with a writing instrument, to Jim. After all, he's always bragging about how he got an A in algebra in high school.

"Jim, I'd like you to rewrite the problem and then solve it. First of all, get someone to call out a number to put in for the question mark."

Jim asks someone in the group to contribute a number. Let's say someone yells out 15. Jim puts that in the equation, and then completes the equation so that it looks like this: (15×4)+34 =

Make sure that he writes it down correctly.

"While you're solving that, Jim, I'm going to build a magic square."

On a separate sheet of paper, you have previously placed a blank square made up of 16 squares, with four rows and four columns.

Since 15 was called out, you add 1 to it, making 16. You enter this number in the lowest left square (Illus. 43). Put the next higher number directly above it. Continue this sequence as shown in Illus. 44.

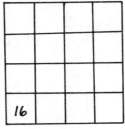

Illus. 43

19	23	27	31
18	22	26	30
17	21	25	29
16	20	24	28

Illus. 44

Quite often you'll finish your magic square before Jim finishes solving the equation, but it really doesn't matter. When you're both done, say, "What's your answer, Jim?" It's 94: (15×4)+34=94.

"There's no doubt, Jim, that if a different number had been put in for that question mark, your answer would have been different, right?" Right.

Shirley is superb at addition, so hand her your diagram, along with a writing instrument.

"Please add up the four corners, Shirley." She does. "What did you get?" She gets 94.

"Add up one of the diagonal rows, please." She gets 94.

"Add up the other diagonal row." She gets 94.

"Add up the four numbers that form a box in the middle." Again 94.

"Undoubtedly, there are many similar combinations," you lie cheerfully. "But let's try something different. Shirley, please circle any one of the numbers." She does so. "Now, cross out the rest of the numbers in that row and in that column." Suppose she circles number 21. Make sure she properly crosses out the other numbers (Illus. 45).

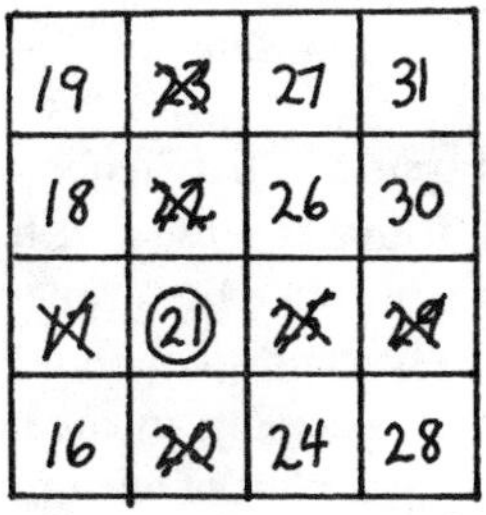

Illus. 45

Have her circle another number, and then cross out all the other numbers in that row and column which have not yet been crossed out. Suppose she chooses 24 (Illus. 46).

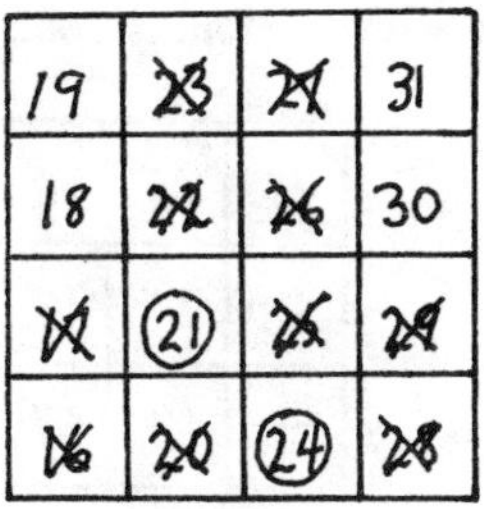

Illus. 46

Have Shirley circle yet another number and again cross out all the other numbers in that row and column which have not yet been crossed out. Let's say she chooses 30 (Illus. 47):

Now, tell her, "One other number remains uncircled, Shirley. Please put a circle around that last number." After she does, say, "Please add up the four circled numbers." She does so.

"Remember, Shirley, you freely selected the numbers to be circled. Is it possible that you ended up with the magic total?" It is possible. The total of the four circled numbers is 94.

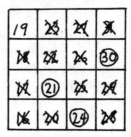

Illus. 47

Why It Works: My guess is that Stephen Tucker worked backward in developing this trick. It makes sense that he might jot down this fairly simple square, and then notice the properties of it—that the corners added to the same number, and so on. But how do you make a trick out of this? One solution is to develop an equation which will yield a number you can work with regardless of what number is chosen by the spectator. Undoubtedly, this involved considerable trial and error.

The second part of the trick is quite ingenious. Let's take a look at another square. Suppose the spectator put in the number 7 for the question mark. You add 1 to this, getting 8. The number in the lowest left corner will be 8, and the other numbers will follow as before (Illus. 48). The four corner numbers add up to 62. And, of course, each diagonal row adds up to 62, and so do the four numbers in the middle.

11	15	19	23
10	14	18	22
9	13	17	21
8	12	16	20

Illus. 48

You're now going to choose a number and eliminate the other numbers in that row and column. So you choose 19 (Illus. 49).

Under the rules, what numbers are left to pick? You could choose 10, 13, and 20. Or 10, 12, and 21. Or 9, 14, and 20. Or 9, 12, and 22. Or 8, 14, and 21. Or 8, 13, and 22. What do you notice about all the possibilities? That's right; they all add up to 43. Together with 19, each one totals 62.

Let's say that your next choice is 13. The square now looks like Illus. 50.

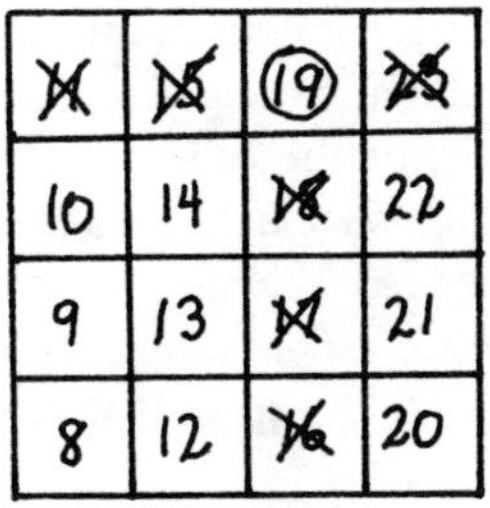

Illus. 49

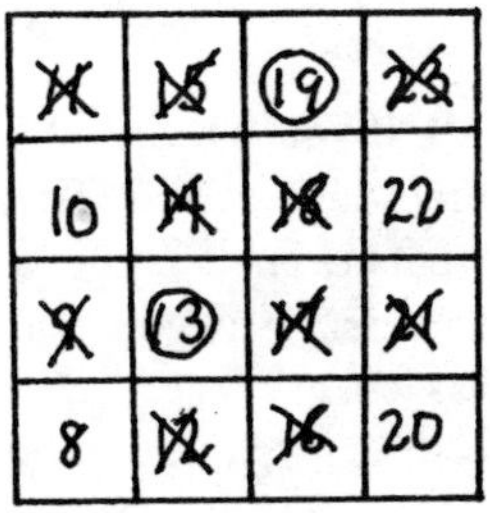

Illus. 50

Notice what your remaining choices are:You may choose either 10 and 20 or 22 and 8. In either instance, the numbers add up to 30. You have already chosen 19 and 13, which total 32. Add 30, and you get 62.

In fact, no matter how you slice it, you get 62. When a square is constructed like this, and you choose numbers in this fashion, you'll always end up with the same number.

So Where's the Money?

A well-known magician came up with an unusual trick using a magic square. The only problem was that it was, in fact, a non-trick. The idea was that the spectator was to randomly choose a square, whereas he was actually forced to choose a particular square. The spectator's instructions told him, step by step, to eliminate every square except the desired one. It seemed to me that this could be improved on.

You'll need playing cards and a coin. (An alternative with pencil and paper is presented in the note at the end.) Remove from the deck A 2 3 4 5 6 7 8 9 of any suit.

Ask Lydia to help you. Explain to the group, "If you don't mind, I'll tell you a story instead of performing a stunt that requires trickery and deceit.

"Once upon a time, Madame Anastasia, that superb psychic, walked into the police station and told the police, 'I've had a vision. Some stolen money is hidden in one of the cabins at the Moldy Motel.' Madame Anastasia had helped the police before, so they asked her to come to the motel with them. She agreed. When they arrived, they discovered that it was a very old motel with nine old cabins."

Deal out the nine cards faceup so that, from Lydia's viewpoint, they look like this:

A	2	3
4	5	6
7	8	9

"Lydia, I'd like to see if you have psychic powers—if you can do as good a job as Madame Anastasia did. These cards represent the nine cabins. The ace represents cabin Number 1, the 2 is cabin Number 2, and so on. Madame Anastasia strolled among the cabins and eliminated them until only one was left.

"I'd like you to do the same thing, following this guide which was provided to me by Madame Anastasia herself."

Set a sheet of paper on the table so that Lydia can read it.

"On the other side of this sheet is the number of the cabin that Madame Anastasia finally decided on. Let's see if you end up with the same one." Hand her the coin. "This coin will represent Madame Anastasia as she wanders around. Start by placing the coin on any one of the cabins." Pause, giving her time to do so. "Then follow the instructions. But first, you have to know what a move is. Wherever the coin is, you can move directly to the left or right, or you can move straight up or straight down. But you can't move at an angle."

The trick will not work unless Lydia starts out on an odd number. If the coin is on an odd number at this point, simply continue. If it's not on an odd number, say, "Would you please make a move, Lydia, so I can be sure I've made myself clear." (Don't say anything like, "I want to make sure you understand." This is somewhat insulting.)

After she makes this move, she has to be on an odd number.

"When you follow the directions, Lydia, you'll end up on a cabin of your choice. First, eliminate the cabin you land on by turning the card facedown. But be sure to keep the coin on it. Then follow Madame Anastasia's directions and eliminate whatever cabin you're told to."

Tell Lydia to follow the directions on the sheet, which should have something like this typed on one side:

MADAME ANASTASIA'S PERSONAL INSTRUCTIONS

Make your move or moves as indicated in the numbered directions below. Eliminate the cabin on which the coin lands by turning the card facedown. Then eliminate the motel you're told to eliminate by turning that card facedown.

You must always land on a motel that has not been eliminated, so make sure you have a safe landing before you actually move the coin.

1) Make 1 move with the coin. Eliminate Cabin 9.
2) Make 2 moves. Eliminate Cabin 5.
3) Make 4 moves. Eliminate Cabin 7.
4) Make 2 moves. Eliminate Cabin 1.

Lydia ends up on Cabin 3. Ask her to turn the sheet of paper over and read the message aloud. She reads: "Congratulations. Madame Anastasia also chose Cabin 3. Unfortunately, no money was there, so she is now reading tea leaves at a small lunch-room in Sydney, Australia."

Why It Works: This is extraordinarily simple. The instructions force the spectator to land on even numbers, which are eliminated. Meanwhile, the directions eliminate all the odd numbers except the number 3.

Note: As I mentioned, the trick can also be done with paper and pencil. Instead of using playing cards, make a 3×3 box with the numbers 1 to 9 enclosed (Illus. 51). Again, the spectator uses a coin, but eliminates cabins by crossing them out with the pencil.

You use the same instruction sheet, but your introductory remarks will vary a little.

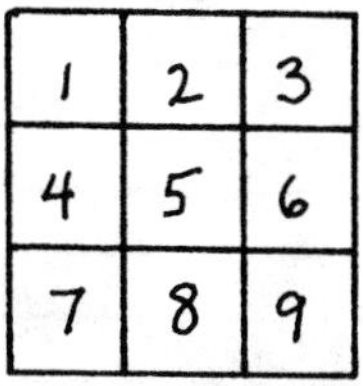

1	2	3
4	5	6
7	8	9

Illus. 51

MASTERY LEVELS CHART & INDEX

Trick	Page	Easy	Harder	Advanced
			Level of Difficulty	
Additional Trick, An	73			*
Age and Address, Please	14		*	
Ah, Yes, I Remember It Well	80			*
All Together Now	65	*		
And the Number Is...	48		*	
As I Recall	82		*	
Birthday Change	10		*	
Children and Other Pets	24		*	
Completely by Chance	58		*	
Dice Are Cast, The	42	*		
Double-Surprise	34			*
Easy Square, An	84	*		
Easy Way, The	19	*		
Five Chosen Cards	26	*		
Getting Along	23	*		
Good Call, A	51	*		
Have a Roll	43		*	
Hummer by Phone	21	*		
Invisible Deck—Again	28		*	
It All Adds Down	63	*		
Little Help, A	52			*
Magician's Choice	55		*	
More Info	12			*
Nickel for Your Thoughts, A	65	*		
Odds or Evens	60		*	
Of an Age	7			*
Old Enough	15	*		
On the Square	87		*	
Phone It In	9	*		
Play the Odds	53	*		
Please State Your City	64	*		
Serial Number Scam	79		*	
Simple Miraskill	38		*	

Level of Difficulty

Trick	Page	Easy	Harder	Advanced
Sly Inference, A	17	*		
Sneaky Serpent, The	66		*	
So Where's the Money?	91		*	
Speedy Adder, The	69			*
Still Hungry?	64	*		
Take Two	44	*		
Talk 'n' Roll	45		*	
Tallying the Future	56	*		
Two Are Better than One	32		*	
Unlucky Seven	30	*		
Working Together	46		*	

ABOUT THE AUTHOR

Bob Longe, a retired English teacher, is an ardent hobbyist. He has charted stocks, played duplicate bridge, and painted. He plays the piano, the tenor banjo, and the ukulele. Inspired by the big stage shows of the great illusionists Blackstone and Dante, he took up magic in the 1930s. He wrote two booklets on card tricks: *The Invisible Deck* was published by the Ireland Magic Company of Chicago; *The Visible Deck* was self-published. Over the years, he has taught magic, particularly card tricks and coin tricks, to dozens of aspiring magicians.

In the late 1970s, Bob wrote, coproduced, and performed in the syndicated radio satire show "Steve Sado, Private Eye." He lives in Rochester Hills,Michigan, with his wife, Betty.